"The premise behind *There Is Still Time* is t
history: Ingenious as our species may be, is
it will take to keep our civilization viable, before it's too late? Peter Seidel
lays out all that ails the Earth in this make-or-break century, and leaves it
to us to decide whether our saga continues, or ends all too soon."
> —**Alan Weisman**, author of *Countdown: Our Last, Best Hope for a
> Future on Earth?* and *The World Without Us*

"There is a lot here that needs to be said. . . . As a species, we are in deep
trouble, and this book helps explain why this is so. Then the question is,
what can we do about it?"
> —**Lester Brown**, founder of the Worldwatch Institute and the Earth
> Policy Institute, author of *Plan B 4.0*

"The author has packed this book with wisdom and insight. It highlights substantial flaws in current institutions, misguided cultural beliefs, and dangerous psychological biases, all of which hold us back from reversing the current trends toward self-destruction."
> —**Mathis Wackernagel**, co-creator of the Ecological Footprint and
> President of the Global Footprint Network

"There is nothing to fear, not even fear. What we need to fear is complacency and ignorance. Anyone reading this book will no longer suffer
from ignorance. This is a potent wake-up call because it rests on facts and
data. Facts and data that tell us not what *will* be, but what *would* be *if . . .*"
> —**Ervin Laszlo**, Founder and President of The Club of Budapest

"Many years of thought, practical work, and reflection are distilled in Peter
Seidel's careful analysis and urgent call to action. The book is wide-ranging
and accessible to the public, yet without any 'dumbing down.' Highly rec-
ommended."
> —**Herman Daly**, one of the founders of the field of ecological econom-
> ics, and author of *Beyond Growth: The Economics of Sustainable De-
> velopment*

"This uniquely structured, crystal-clear book is the culmination of long-term, deep thinking about the prospect of the human race to escape the catastrophic outcomes of a bloating economy. *There Is Still Time* should be required reading for policy makers, civic leaders, and most of all in the 'sustainability' courses cropping up in college curricula."

> —**Brian Czech**, President, Center for Advancement of the Steady State Economy, author of *Supply Shock: Economic Growth at the Crossroads* and the *Steady State Solution*

"This book combines admirable honesty about the human predicament with suggestions for regaining hope by focusing on what is realistically possible in the available time."

> —**Robert Engelman**, former President Worldwatch Institute

"Seidel is a true child of the Enlightenment. A man who believes that men can think and act rationally."

> —**Jeffery van Davis**, award-winning filmmaker, *Only God Can Save Us*

"Seidel's blend of pessimism and idealism brings intellectual heft to this unconventional approach so that we might 'move beyond our current stalemate and make real progress towards sustainability.' . . . An astute look at the many negative influences currently shaping our world, along with ideas to overcome them."

> —**Kirkus Review**

THERE IS STILL TIME

To Look at the Big Picture…and Act

By Peter Seidel

With an overview of our planet today by Gary Gardner

360° Editions • Cincinnati, Ohio

Published by:

360° Editions
5300 Hamilton Avenue, Suite 1403
Cincinnati, OH 45224

Editor: Carol Cartaino, White Oak Editions, Seaman, OH
Text Designer: Christine Brooks
Cover design: George Lois

ISBN: 978-0-578-16975-0

CIP data available upon request

FEB − 5 2016

"We have created a Star Wars civilization with Stone Age emotions,

medieval institutions, and godlike technology."

— Edward O. Wilson, 2012[1]

Dedicated to those who will live in the world that we leave them.

CONTENTS

PART ONE: A CALL TO ACTION

1. From My Balcony   3

The view is a fine one, but many disturbing realities underlie it. We are largely disconnected from the natural world that supports us, and give little thought to how our actions affect it. We tend to see the world as pieces, but this chapter makes it clear that the time has come—in fact, is way overdue—to put those pieces together and see the big picture.

2. A Look at Ourselves   12

A quick overview of our uninspiring record as a species—how we have treated one another, and the planet we depend on.

3. The Many Problems We Face Today   16

We are faced today with two sets of problems that affect our well-being, those of the environment, and those embedded in our very nature, war and violence for example. We are the root cause of both. We ignore these roots and go for the obvious, trying to deal with problems on superficial levels, one by one—and not very well. As a result, we are in danger of bringing about our own demise. A review of all of the factors, environmental and circumstantial, social and purely human, that contribute to this, and are part of the giant headache of interacting issues we need to work our way out of as quickly as we can.

PART TWO: OUR PLANET TODAY
by Gary Gardner

A concise, comprehensive, up-to-date survey of what is actually happening in the world today, in nine essential areas.

FOREWORD

It is sometimes said that we must not depict dangers that are on the horizon, for that will just create fear in people and result in helplessness and paralysis. That may apply to some individuals, but not to the human family as a whole. Our family—this remarkable species—has enormous and as yet untapped resources at its disposal. Whether we call it a collective consciousness, a species survival instinct, or the emerging noosphere, the fact is that there is something emerging in the world: a new mentality, a revived spirit, a reborn vision. That is our greatest and best hope, and it is what we need to address and reinforce. Peter Seidel's book does precisely that. It does not tell us that we will go under; it tells us that we *could*—if we fail to live up to the challenge of our collective survival. That challenge is being met by the new cultures emerging at the creative margins of almost every society today. It needs to be strengthened, and there is nothing better for that than a kind of constructive vaccine: a bit of the foretaste of the dangers that would await us *if*....

The best recipe for creating a better world tomorrow is a crisis today. But this does not have to be a lived, an experienced crisis; it could be a foreseen, "perceived" crisis. A crisis *if*.... And that perception is precisely what Seidel is projecting. We should consider his message and act on it, with confidence that we can rise to the challenge. We can, because the human spirit is capable of it. Seidel believes that it is, and so do I.

We need not fear what lies ahead—what we need to fear is complacency and ignorance. Anyone reading this book will no longer suffer from ignorance. This is a potent wake-up call because it rests on facts and data. Facts and data that tell us not what *will* be, but what *would* be *if*.... What with some common sense—some uncommonly good common sense—*could* be. And what really *will* be—if we wake up and act.

—Ervin Laszlo
Founder and President of the Club of Budapest

PREFACE

In 1958 I read geochemist Harrison Brown's 1954 book, *The Challenge of Man's Future: an Inquiry Concerning the Condition of Man During the Years That Lie Ahead.* It left me with much to think about, and changed the course of not only my personal but my professional life as an architect and urban planner. In time it led to this book. I thank him for that.

Disturbed by humanity's indifference to all of the evidence clearly showing that we are harming our planet, in 1998 I published a book that looked at this problem, *Invisible Walls: Why We Ignore the Damage We Inflict on Our Planet...and Ourselves.* Since then, environmental damage has only grown worse and major segments of our population and governments have become more resistant to doing anything significant about it. Taking a broader look at why we do not live in harmony with our planet nor with each other, I collected ideas from my reading and personal observations and organized them into a manuscript. The more I collected, the more clearly I saw our overall situation, and the more depressed I became. I began to wonder whether what I was writing would serve a useful purpose and whether it should ever be published. Knowing that some environmentalists strongly believe that we must always present a positive message to the public added weight to this thought.

On the other hand, it is clear that if we continue on our current course our future will be grim indeed. Facing the dismal facts might get us to think and change. On this thought, I felt pressed to move ahead, however I wanted input from individuals whose thinking I greatly respect. I sent my manuscript to a few of them for their reaction. I am grateful to Ervin Laszlo, who besides encouraging me offered to write the Foreword, and to Lester Brown, Mathis Wackernagel, Robert Engleman, Robert Dietz, and Brian Czech. They all encouraged me to publish, and so I have.

PART ONE

A Call to Action

Chapter One

FROM MY BALCONY

As I gaze out from my thirteenth floor balcony, it's hard to believe that I'm near the center of a metropolitan area of more than two million people. Most of what I see is lush green. Nearly all of the buildings are obscured by the trees that cover the tops of what appear to be hills, or are tucked away in valleys hidden from me by wooded ridges. To my left, on top of what appears to be a long wooded hill, is what looks like an Italian hill town with high-rise buildings rather than fortifications. Straight ahead, a high-power electric line leads off to the west where beyond the horizon two columns of white smoke ascend to the sky.

As the sun sets this scene changes. Darkness now hides the trees, leaving lights blinking out from here and there. The "town" in the valley is now ablaze with light, as is the "Italian hill town" way to the left. Below it, streaming up and down the valley, is a parade of lights moving in both directions—an interstate! One wonders why all those cars and trucks from up there want to go down there, and those from down there are going up there. It would save a lot of time, wear and tear, and energy if most of them just stayed where they were. And what about the energy needed to keep all those lights I see on and the air conditioners that are running to keep us cool on this hot night? I know that the power plants just over the horizon, producing the towers of smoke I saw, are being fed day by day by the removal of mountaintops in West Virginia and eastern Kentucky to keep all of this, including my computer, going.

All of the people out there, like myself, are linked to things we cannot see. Our genes and culture are gifts from the past and we are making the future right now as we go about our daily business. We obtain what we need, or just desire, such as food, water, minerals, energy, the oxygen in

Figure 1. Changing landscape: mountaintop removal and strip mining. Photo by Vivian Stockman, www.ohvec.org

the air, and the flowers we buy in January from other parts of the world. In turn we expel what we do not need or want.

Unnoticed by us, those vehicles out there are consuming a valuable and limited resource produced millions of years ago. The carbon dioxide they spew into the atmosphere is helping to change the Earth's climate. And those power plants are also disgorging huge amounts of carbon dioxide, as well as sulfur dioxide, nitrogen oxide, particulate matter, and mercury up into the atmosphere.

We eat hamburgers made from beef grazed on lands cleared from tropical forests that once contained vast amounts of carbon. When those forests are burned, that carbon is released into the atmosphere as CO_2. In addition, the animals destined for our hamburgers produce huge amounts of methane, which is twenty-three times more powerful than CO_2 as a greenhouse gas. The jets that bring us grapes from Chile and shrimp from Thailand create more of these gases. And then there is what we discard. While much of it gets stowed away out of sight nearby, or dumped into waterways and carried to the ocean, some of the most toxic substances find a home in the bodies of the world's poor who don't have access to clean water. We have regulations, laws, police, and armies trying to protect us and keep order among us, however our efforts to protect our planet and other forms of life fall far short. As we shall see, we can do better.

Disconnection

We are part of nature; however we do not feel it nor live accordingly. Instead we see ourselves connected to the worlds of technology, money, consumerism, and entertainment. A mere one hundred years ago, most people knew where what they needed came from, and to a lesser degree where what they discarded went. Most of what we consumed came from nearby, while human and animal waste was returned to the soil to replenish it. Today, although waste is generated everywhere we are (and there is a lot of it!), it is kept out of sight. Nevertheless, it weighs heavily on the environment, poisoning the air, land, and our water supplies, while leaving soil deprived of essential nutrients and organic matter. Today, we are mentally and often physically disconnected from the root sources of the food, energy, and materials we consume, and where the waste we produce ends up. We do not normally care about what we do not see or feel. When we buy milk or strawberries at a supermarket, we don't know where they come from, nor do we care.

Traditionally (and today in farmers' markets) we purchased food from the people who produced it. Not much more than fifty years ago most of us could walk to a grocery store to shop for food, and often stores would deliver right to our homes. Since then the nearby grocery has been replaced by a neighborhood supermarket, and that has been replaced by a larger supermarket farther away that we could not walk to. And even that has been replaced by ever greater supermarkets that dazzle the buyer and save distribution costs for the merchant, but require ever more driving, parking lots, and roads for us to get there. The dazzle has blinded most of us to the cost to the environment and cost in time and money to ourselves. We are turning farmland that will soon be needed for feeding people into pavement and rooftops, and consuming ever more polluting fossil fuels to keep food on our tables.

When we buy a diamond or gold ring we don't see the cruelties imposed on the African miners who dig these treasures out, some of whom are children, and some slaves, nor the corruption in their countries caused by warlords and criminal mine operators. Likewise, when we jump in our car to go somewhere, we fail to connect this to the melting of glaciers in

Figure 2. Boy diamond miner in Zimbabwe. Photo by Robin Hammond/Panos

the Himalayas, nor do we consider the fact that the money we spend at the pumps is helping Saudi Wahhabis fund religious schools where fundamentalist Islam is taught along with hate, and where future terrorists are bred.

We spend most of our lives in artificial environments, see attractively packaged food coming from supermarkets, and are oblivious to the places and people who produced it. We vacation in far-off places we often know better than the countryside around our community and maybe our own backyards. Such is the world we know. In it, we are separated from food production and waste disposal, and from most natural sights, sounds, and smells of the world that keeps us alive. While many Native Americans saw themselves as being a part of nature, most modern Europeans and North Americans see technology and the economy as the foundations of our well-being, land as a commodity to be bought and sold, and nature as a resource to be exploited.

Our planet, and even our species, has been here for a long time, but for us, reality is "now." Because we fail to see time on a larger scale everything in the scene before us seems just the same as it was yesterday. But it is not. We don't notice that today there are 218,000 more people on our planet than yesterday, or that 15,000 children will die today as a result of malnutrition; 67,000 acres of arable land will be seriously degraded or abandoned to agriculture; 33,000 acres of forest will be obliterated; desertification will claim nearly 3.9 square miles more of land in China; and water tables around the world will continue to drop.[2] While many Americans have heard such facts, few of us give them more than a fleeting thought, or grasp their significance. They just don't sink in.

Merely to maintain the status quo, which includes a huge number of people living in utter misery, the Global Footprint Network estimates it would take 1.5 planets like ours to renewably produce all the resources humanity demands and to absorb its CO_2 emissions. Even if everyone lived like Europeans, who consume and pollute a lot less than we Americans do, we would require the resources of almost 5 planets to reach sustainability.[3] One can live off of the principal of a bank account for a while; likewise we can get by with exploiting our planet and overlooking the plight of the unfortunate for a few more decades. And since we don't personally see or feel what is happening, we are bothered little.

Few people think about where this is leading. While we are totally dependent on the natural world, we are continually diverting our thoughts ever further from it and becoming ever more connected with the artificial world we have created, such as fast food restaurants, automobiles, TV, the Internet, and iPhones.

We see the world as pieces

As a boy I enjoyed standing on street corners in my hometown of Milwaukee and imagining what the scene before me would have been like fifty years before, and would be like fifty years in the future. I was disturbed by all the automobiles I saw around me burning up what I knew was a limited resource that would be needed for ambulances and fire engines in the future. These thoughts and concerns have not left me. My interest in connecting things and events found a place when I became interested in architecture and city planning. I enjoyed and saw the importance of seeing buildings, cities, and all of their systems as wholes and evaluating their influence on people as well as how they would fit into and affect their surroundings. Almost everything in our world is in some way connected to most everything else.

We humans do not view or see the world as an integrated whole. Instead we observe it as if we are looking though a tube focusing on one tiny piece of it at a time. Many of us are very skilled and knowledgeable in one or a few small areas. Our competence in that often makes us think we understand a lot more than we do. By focusing their attention on very small pieces of reality, exceptional individuals have developed an incredible knowledge about genes, strings, and dark matter, and developed remarkable capabilities in fields like nanotechnology and space exploration. Stepping back and looking at how we are utilizing this knowledge in dealing with one another and our planet, we can see that it is sometimes wonderful and other times awful. What we too often have is a collection of good parts put together in bad ways.

Our technology gives us an overwhelming impact on our surroundings, which can be disastrous when not used wisely for the good of the world today and that of the future. The combination of ignorance, arrogance, and technology is leading us towards serious trouble.

The planet's biosphere we interact with is an integrated whole whose parts work together to maintain the milieu we live in. This life-sustaining environment and its support systems, such as the carbon cycle, which circulates carbon between living matter and the atmosphere, are kept in balance by two things. One is called ecology, and the other is what James Lovelock calls "Gaia." Ecology maintains population balance between the many species of plants and animals that inhabit the earth. Gaia, by interactions between life forms and the inert materials of our planet, helps maintain the conditions (atmospheric composition, temperature, air pressure, humidity, etc.), in which life can thrive. If Gaia did not keep levels of atmospheric oxygen lower than twenty-one percent, animals could not burn enough food energy to function properly. If the oxygen content were higher, vegetation would burst into flame. Small amounts of ammonia in the atmosphere neutralize sulfuric and nitric acids there, which would kill vegetation if they fell to the earth dissolved in raindrops. If our planet's atmospheric pressure dropped significantly we would explode.

Things are not only connected with each other in the present, but to things in the past and the future as well. To truly understand the way things are and what is happening we have to understand our history and evolutionary past. Sadly, as links in a chain and beneficiaries of our past and present, we show little concern for those who will follow.

Some of our failures to see connections are obvious, yet we ignore them. Continuous population increase and economic growth on a finite planet is impossible. Nevertheless, questioning unending economic growth is taboo. Even many environmentalists won't do that. Malaria is a dangerous and debilitating disease; however controlling it without addressing population growth is creating terrible conditions in Africa. Prohibiting the distribution of means for birth control as some nations and organizations insist on doing makes no sense, but they keep at it.

We have trouble recalling, connecting, and utilizing information, significant as it might be, that is not clearly related to a particular situation. Should they think about it, most economists, politicians, and businesspeople would know that neither our nation's population nor its economy can grow indefinitely. Yet when these things fail to grow, they register alarm. While they are understandably concerned about the problems that accompany a stagnant economy, they totally ignore the consequences of perpetual expansion. It does not occur to them that many current problems are the inevitable result of past "successful" growth. We may value how much a person knows, but usually show little concern for their ability to make any but the most obvious connections. People who know a lot about a particular subject and can present themselves well often gain responsible positions in society—even though they show no interest in important relationships between things. This is serious when these people make far-reaching decisions that affect the future.

We have trouble getting down to the basic causes of our environmental problems, as obvious as they and their interactions are. In the 1970s Paul Ehrlich and John Holdren presented a simple formula called IPAT. IPAT stands for: $I = P \times A \times T$, where I = impact, P = population, A = affluence (consumption per capita), and T = technology. If everything stays the same but the world population doubles, humanity's impact on the planet doubles. Similarly, if everything stays the same but personal consumption and pollution double, humanity's impact on the planet doubles. On the other hand if everything is done twice as efficiently, humanity's impact on the planet is cut in half. Although this equation is simple and clear enough, with our inclination to focus on pieces, we don't seem to grasp it, or we ignore it. This is not surprising as it forces us to deal with uncomfortable issues. It's easy to suggest improving technology, but seriously discussing population reduction is taboo, and who dares to suggest that we consume less?

Limiting our thinking to pieces pays off. Focusing one's knowledge, expertise, and efforts in a narrow area avoids distractions, simplifies work, brings one success in one's field, and can make one famous or a multimillionaire. Generalists with a broad vision, who see the big picture with its problems, often find it difficult to come up with uncomplicated answers because there may be none. They often have trouble finding employment that matches their abilities in a world that does not value them, so they are often ignored and left out of important decisions affecting us all.

Tunnel thinking affects a wide range of activities, including politics and the behavior of governments. Individuals and groups who focus on single issues such as preventing birth control or abortion, or control of firearms, and disregard other concerns have a huge impact on politics. To maintain their position or gain political support, some politicians let these issues overrun more serious concerns, such as the environment, in order to stay in office and satisfy their backers. This accounts for a wide range of irrational action followed by serious consequences.

No one at the helm

Ant colonies, beehives, groups of human hunter-gatherers, and our cities and nations are organized at various levels. With all the remarkable technology we have developed, the information that is available, and the organization we have put in place, it would be reasonable to think that what is taking place in this city around me and what lies beyond it, makes sense. As a child I thought that "grown-ups" were wise, understood everything, and knew what was best for all of us. I have grown up and have learned that there is no wise person, group, or organization that is managing what is essential for us in this world where we have broken down the barriers that once kept us in balance with our environment.

What's going on out there is simply driven by uncoordinated primitive human drives, at times tempered by reason. All of this activity is a combination of many unconnected, uncoordinated efforts mostly working to meet short-term wants and needs. Most people focus their attention and concerns on the well-being of their family, close associates, and themselves, giving little thought to the overall good or the future.

Political leaders, democratic or autocratic, who should have their hands on what society is doing, give most of their attention to maintaining their position instead—although they may give the appearance that their real concerns lie elsewhere. Even when well intentioned and trying their best, they have limited time and energy to deal with much beyond the everyday needs of conflicting interests and their constituents. Traditionalists may say that this pursuit of self-interest is Adam Smith's "invisible hand" working as self-organization for the overall good. Conventional economists, bankers, business leaders, and politicians laud this for putting and keeping us on track for economic growth.

There is no entity examining and controlling our impact on the planet, nor do government leaders or most people discuss this or see the need for it. We plunge ahead ignoring warnings that all is not OK. We are essentially a mindless mass with tremendous power in our hands.

Today we are like a bull in a china shop, seemingly unaware of the havoc we are creating. We all know a lot of what I will be describing in the following chapters, but we tend to view it in pieces, so we don't see the scope of the problem, the big picture. To get that, we must put the pieces together and look at the whole, which I will try to do here.

Chapter Two

A LOOK AT OURSELVES

In order to fully comprehend what is happening in the world today, the rapidly evolving problems humanity faces, and to be able to deal with them, we must look at our situation realistically—without illusions. We are clearly on a path headed for catastrophe, and although there is abundant information about what's wrong and what we can do about it, we are failing to respond to it in a rational, responsible way. In looking for an explanation of this, it is clear that the problem lies within ourselves as human beings.

OUR TENURE ON PLANET EARTH

In order to understand how we got to where we are, it will help to look at our past.

Misuse of Earth

Until humans took up agriculture around ten thousand years ago, they lived within the confines of a stable ecologic niche; a very few of us still do in remote areas such as the Amazon. Nature's ways of keeping populations balanced are brutal: limited food supplies, predators, parasites, and disease. Over time exceptional individuals found ways to overcome disagreeable constraints on our niche such as these. Agriculture and other innovations, and later modern medicine enabled our population to grow enormously, putting it at odds with other forms of life. During the last several centuries further technological advances have accelerated the expansion of our niche and our impact on the planet. While many constraints have been pushed aside, they have not been replaced by self-control, except in some limited areas. We are plunging ahead into the unknown at an ever-increasing speed, driven by primitive human drives, giving little thought to where we are headed.

We have not only squandered irreplaceable natural resources, and polluted the land, the water, and the atmosphere, but poor farming practices have stripped land of its productive topsoil and seriously damaged food production. This happened earlier in such places as ancient Greece, North Africa, China, and pre-Columbian Central America, and over-salinization ruined irrigation systems in Mesopotamia and the Indus Valley. Rampant population growth, deforestation, and topsoil destruction caused the Mayan and Easter Island civilizations to collapse.

Not having learned from experiences like these, we are using farming methods today that are seriously damaging our planet's ability to produce adequate food on into the future. We are doing other reckless things like causing species extinction and altering the climate of our planet. We are now changing the environment so rapidly that many species cannot adapt fast enough to survive. While figures are hard to arrive at, we may be losing species between 1,000 and 10,000 times faster than the natural extinction rate. Thousands of plant and animal species are disappearing, and soon there will not be enough land left to support large carnivores in the wild.

We have already obliterated many species of life and many more will soon disappear as our population grows and we increase our burden on

Figure 3. Cleared forest in Sumatra. Photo © Melvinas Priananda, Greenpeace

the Earth. Looking at the overall picture of what we are doing to our planet it is clear that we are destroying our own future—unless we change.

Hostilities towards each other

While the damage we have inflicted on our planet was not intentional, much of how we have dealt with other human beings was. Killing and warfare over territory, differing beliefs, and for revenge date back to the earliest human societies. William James wrote, "History is a bath of blood.[4]" Religion, which many see as the source of human ethics and civility, has often led people to terrible violence. For the Romans cruelty to animals and humans in public gladiatorial spectacles and torturous executions was a form of entertainment.

Much of recorded history is the history of war and conflict. Wars between chiefdoms, tribes, and states have gone on as far as we can look back in history. As David J. Morris noted in his book *The Evil Hours,* "...the historian Will Durant calculated that there have been only twenty-nine years in all of human history when there wasn't a war going on somewhere in the world."

During wars, defeating an enemy was often not enough—cities were leveled, populations killed or enslaved, and women raped. We do not

Figure 4. Scene below deck of a slave ship headed to Brazil in the 1820s. From Johann Moritz Rugendas' book *Voyage Pittoresque dans le Bresil.* Wikimedia Commons

have to look beyond the Bible to get a sense of this. Deuteronomy 20:16, "But of the cities of these people which the Lord thy God doth give thee for an inheritance, thou shalt save alive nothing that breatheth." At times the killings were exceedingly brutal.

Many cities in Asia, Europe, Africa, and the New World were walled to protect people from other people. Some of the greatest technical innovations humans have made were developed for weaponry and defenses.

Slavery existed in almost every civilization and society, including Sumer, ancient Egypt, ancient China, the Akkadian Empire, Assyria, ancient India, ancient Greece, the Roman Empire, the Islamic Caliphate, the Hebrews in Palestine, and the pre-Columbian civilizations of the Americas. Russia's more than twenty-three million privately held serfs were freed from their lords by an edict of Alexander II in 1861. State-owned serfs were emancipated in 1866. Slaves in the United States were not granted their freedom until 1862. By 1900, slaves comprised up to one-third of Ethiopia's population. Emperor Haile Selassie officially abolished slavery in 1942. While generally illegal, slavery persists in the world today, even under cover in the United States. Some owners managed their slaves humanely; nonetheless they were the property of their owners and were often treated with extreme severity with no recourse.

Chapter Three ∽

THE MANY PROBLEMS WE FACE TODAY

We are faced with serious threats to the future of our planet and to our species, however we are addressing them far from adequately. Today many ongoing threats continue and grow rapidly in intensity, while new ones continue to appear. Many of these are caused by our efforts to improve our lives. Some of these problems are environmental, and others lie within human society. Some of what I describe here is my own observations, but most of it has been pointed out by scientists and other knowledgeable experts.

IN THE NATURAL WORLD

I find it hard to believe that there are now more than 3½ times as many people on this planet as when I was born in 1926. Growing numbers of people demanding ever more things and creating ever more waste and pollution are placing rapidly increasing burdens on our planet. Our limitless thirst for fossil fuels is leading to the depletion of irreplaceable resources and bringing about climate change. This in turn produces more extreme weather conditions, rising sea levels, and ocean acidification, resulting in a great reduction of fauna and flora there. Water contamination and shortages, deforestation, loss of cropland, soil erosion, and the deterioration of ecosystems threaten food production for an ever-growing human population. All of this forces mass migration of people from areas that can no longer support and sustain them.

Today, through the publication of regular updates on scientific research, we are learning that many of these problems are worse than we had previously thought. For example, U.S. Department of Energy figures revealed that 2010 levels of greenhouse gases were higher than the worst-case scenario outlined by climate experts just four years before. Also, in 2010 we learned that stocks of phytoplankton had decreased by forty percent since 1950, most likely as a result of global warming.[5] Phytoplankton is the foundation, the starting point, for all the oceans' food chains. This will have grave consequences for life in the oceans and for humankind. Recent data have shown that Arctic glaciers and ice coverage are disappearing and ocean acidification has been increasing much faster than previously predicted.

In order to keep Part One of this book focused on ourselves, on why we are harming Earth and ourselves and failing to deal with either of these things effectively, I have asked Gary Gardner, Senior Fellow at the Worldwatch Institute, to produce an up-to-date survey of what is happening. You will find it in Part Two, with contributions from ecologist Brian Czech, president of the Center for the Advancement of the Steady State Economy, and material supplied by Mathis Wackernagel, co-creator of the Ecological Footprint and President of Global Footprint Network. There are sections on Population, Consumption, Energy, Food and Cropland, Water, the Oceans, Biodiversity, Climate Change, the impact of Current World Economies, and our Ecological Footprint. Together they read like a very short book. Reading this will give you an overview of what we are doing to our planet—a concise yet comprehensive view of our current environmental problems.

IN THE HUMAN-MADE WORLD

Hostilities and aggression

Most people desire a world of peace and cooperation, yet today our world is filled with violence, causing massive human suffering, economic havoc, and environmental damage. But there is evidence that things were once worse. Jared Diamond, whose expertise spans a number of subject areas, makes an interesting comment on the behavior towards strangers in the indigenous New Guinea societies in which he worked. "Should you happen to meet an unfamiliar person in the forest, of course you would try to kill him or else run away; our modern custom of just saying hello and starting a friendly chat would be suicidal."[6] Fortunately we have moved beyond that.

In *The Better Angels of Our Nature: Why Violence Has Declined*,"[7] psy-chologist Steven Pinker presents clear evidence that despite what takes place today, the world is actually much less violent than it was in the past. He points out that as people join together into ever larger units leading up to our nation-states today with many international agreements and global trade, cooperation becomes more important. Although violence is still far too common, most governments and businesses depend on and promote peace. Nevertheless, Pinker shows that there is still ample room to im-prove our behavior.

Some countries are saddled with ruthless leaders who terrorize their own people and threaten world peace—North Korea is an extreme exam-ple. It is difficult to deal with this problem. We also have to contend with broken-down states such as Somalia where chaos reigns, and people are victimized by ruthless gangs and warlords. States like Pakistan are havens for international terrorists and criminals, and in places like Yemen, which lacks any political stability, overpopulation is outstripping the country's ability to provide clean water and adequate food. Unfortunately, the world does not have a system to deal with antisocial leaders, some on the verge of insanity. As time passes, diminishing resources such as food and land will lead to new conflicts between nations.

Hostilities and economic crises divert attention and resources away from critical needs like environmental problems, education, reducing in-equality, and introducing a more stable, equitable economic system. Ac-cording to the Friends Committee for National Legislation, of each dol-lar of federal income tax Americans paid in 2011, the government spent about thirty-nine cents for current and past wars.

Genocide

Genocide sounds like something from the past that should no longer be with us; but it is. During and after World War I the Ottomans brutally tried to cleanse their country of Armenians, killing 600,000–1,800,000. During the Second World War the Nazis initiated a program of geno-cide to exterminate six million Jews and other "undesirables" in Europe. In 1994 an estimated 500,000–1,000,000 Tutsis were killed by Hutus in Rwanda, often with machetes. In 2003, Sinafasi Makelo, a representative of Mbuti Pygmies, told the UN that during the Congo Civil War, Pygmies were being hunted down and eaten as though they were game animals.

Figure 5. Dr. Fritz Klein, a doctor at the camp, stands amongst corpses in Mass Grave 3 at Bergen-Belsen concentration camp in Germany. Imperial War Museum

Farmers in Dafur may still be attacked by horse-riding herders supported by the Sudanese government.

Terrorism

Some dispossessed and impoverished peoples without the resources to wage war see terrorism as their only weapon against the powerful, and there are fanatical religious believers who see it as their duty to attack those with different beliefs. Aided by modern weapons and the Internet, terrorists, often willing to die for their cause, are hard to find and defeat. This has forced society to move beyond traditional ways of doing things and take extreme precautions at airports, government buildings, and oth-

Figure 6. The World Trade Center ablaze with the Statue of Liberty in the foreground. Few of us think of the consequences had the fourth plane hit the Capitol or the White House. User 9/11 Photos on Flickr.com, under Creative Commons License (https://creativecommons.org/licenses/by 2.0 deed.en)

er public spaces, resulting in substantial inconvenience, government surveillance, and cost. Terrorism is affecting how governments and people relate to each other. The availability of very powerful weaponry has also made it easier for deranged individuals to create havoc.

While crises come and go, the causes of terrorism and easily accessible weapons are not likely to go away. Governments influenced by different beliefs, values, and levels of corruption make sane and truly thoughtful responses to the problem difficult. While governments do the obvious thing of searching out and going after terrorists, and take measures to impede them, they make too little effort to understand and deal with causes, leaving extremists to breed future terrorists among the young. This is the case with the Islamic State of Iraq (ISIS), which as I write has become more than just a terrorist organization as it has gained control over a significant amount of territory in Iraq and Syria.

The dangerous weapons we have today

Clubs, spears, and bows and arrows can do great damage to individuals; however, they cannot harm our planet. Today we have stored chemicals,

Agent Orange for example, that can devastate entire landscapes and nuclear weapons that can bring on a nuclear winter. The Cold War ended in 1991, at which time the Soviet Union and the United States had huge stockpiles of nuclear weapons. Although reductions were made, these weapons were not abandoned. Nineteen years later, in 2010, Barack Obama and Dmitry Medvedev signed a treaty reducing the number of operational strategic nuclear weapons from 2,200 to 1,550. And this was between two countries at peace with each other for over twenty years! Of course there are other countries with nuclear weapons to worry about, but looking back at Hiroshima, what kind of logic demands that we retain 1,550 of these bombs, some of which may be nearly 600 times (my own calculation) more powerful than the one that destroyed Hiroshima? Having visited Hiroshima and its museum, and viewed films of the city's destruction, it is beyond my comprehension how the use of any of these weapons can be found acceptable, or from the perspective of a tyrant, how using half a dozen would leave a world that he or she would be able to govern. The development, production, and maintenance of such weapons diverts funds and resources from human needs and protecting the environment.

Our economic predicament

We have an economic system that just to stay where it is depends on perpetual growth in a finite space. In the early 1970s our planet passed beyond the point of environmental sustainability (see Ecological Footprint in Part Two). Still business, government, and almost all the rest of us call for more growth. It seems to me that a fifth grader would know that can't work. To get out of our current recession and return to growth, businesses and government believe they must lay off people from areas such as education, scientific research, environmental protection, the arts, and health care. So some things do not get done while some people have nothing to do. We are not making an effort to solve this dilemma because we hold our economic system to be sacrosanct, no matter how ridiculous the results.

Communism has fallen far behind capitalism in producing prosperity. Capitalism does very well at producing goods and services, however it ignores the limitations of our planet and the needs of the less fortunate. It is now driving us along a path toward inevitable collapse. While people are being laid off, businesspeople are striving for ever greater productivity per worker. This means that when and if the recession ends, per capita production, consumption, waste, and damage to nature will have to increase significantly just to keep people employed. Economists, politicians, the media, and nearly all of the rest of us repeatedly say our big problem today is the economy, and are blind to what is happening to the environment.

Vulnerability

With little thought given to the future, contemporary society is progressively making itself more vulnerable to a variety of events by increasing its dependence on limited natural resources, inexpensive energy and transportation, complex technology requiring people capable of understanding and maintaining it, and on a stable climate, environment, and political systems. Our vulnerability reaches into many areas such as health, with the current development of bacteria immune to antibiotics, and a worldwide food system requiring dependable transportation and supplies of chemicals essential for it. We give little thought to what can happen if catastrophes overlap, coincide with a war, or the more negative aspects of our behavior come to the fore during a breakdown of some kind. It would be wise to give our vulnerabilities a serious look.

Our dependence on electricity. Contemporary society, particularly urban areas, simply cannot function without electricity. Without it people depending on systems such as subways cannot move about. Those with cars would find driving a disaster without traffic signals and streetlights, and be in for a surprise when they discovered that gas stations could not pump fuel from their underground tanks. Heating, cooling, and ventilation systems, and elevators in high-rise buildings would soon stop. (As an architect I once worked on an office building under construction in Tulsa, Oklahoma. The air conditioning went off and the building had to be evacuated within two hours as windows could not be opened.) Without electricity, water could not be pumped to upper floors of buildings, leaving people thirsty and sewage piling up. Food stores would be dark, and refrigerated food would start to spoil. Buildings with backup generators would be OK—for a while.

Unguarded electric power grids are prime targets for physical or cyber attacks by terrorists, overload, and natural threats such as Earth and solar storms. The geomagnetic disturbance of 1859 referred to as "the Carrington Event" induced currents so powerful that telegraph lines, towers, and stations caught fire at a number of places around the world.[8] In 1989, a severe solar storm induced powerful electric currents in grid wiring that fried a main power transformer in the HydroQuebec system, causing a cascading grid failure that knocked out power to six million customers for nine hours. Such transformers cost well over a million dollars each, and there was a three-year waiting list for new ones. A massive solar storm could destroy most of the Earth's transformers. This would threaten all planetary life, as grids are needed to cool spent fuel rods at nuclear power plants. We and our governments register little concern for these seeming unlikely but very real possibilities.

Cyber dangers. A major computer virus, malware, worm, logic bomb, rigged chips, cyber attack, or cyber war between nations could create havoc with anything connected to the Internet. Communications, power grids, global positioning systems, financial, government, military, scientific, and medical records, proprietary information and personal data storage and transactions are vulnerable. The list goes on. It is hard to imagine how devastating this could be for a country like the United States which is now dependent on these systems for our everyday lives, our businesses, our government, and to defend ourselves. When attacked, we may not be able to find out who is behind it. Whereas nations and city-states were once protected by walls, and by various other forms of defenses against aircraft and even missiles, a cyber attack can reach anywhere. Governments and businesses acknowledge and are very aware of these dangers. However, considering their lack of imagination and their penchant for short-term solutions, can we count on them to look at the full extent of the risks and the costs it can take to avoid them, which may even require giving up some of the conveniences and things we like so much? And we may not have the money, time, or talent to be able to deal with the complexity that effective counter-measures would involve.

Water and fossil fuels. We are not only vulnerable to short-term happenings, but to the slow changes we are not preparing for. Both surface and groundwater are essential for human use, agriculture, and industry, however shortages are appearing and water sources are becoming more polluted. This is creating national and international conflicts that will only grow significantly worse.

Fossil fuels are rapidly becoming depleted, and without liquid fuels airplanes would become impractical and ground transportation would become very expensive. The production of ethanol is already competing with the growing of food for humans. In his book, *Storms of my Grandchildren*, James Hansen, adjunct professor in the Department of Earth and Environmental Sciences at Columbia University, and until he resigned in 2013, the

Figure 7. Canadian tar sands mine. Photo by Jiri Rezac/Polaris

head of the NASA Goddard Institute for Space Studies in New York City, warns, "I've come to conclude that if we burn all reserves of oil, gas, and coal, there is a substantial chance we will initiate the runaway greenhouse. If we also burn the tar sand and tar shale, I believe the Venus syndrome [a hot, lifeless planet] is a dead certainty."[9] To obtain natural gas and petroleum through fracking we're pumping huge amounts of badly needed water with toxins added into the ground and rapidly mining the tar sands. None of this seems to bother most people, nor most of those in power.

Without fossil fuels, the feedstock for our plastics industry, we will have to resort to using metals, wood, or what? High-yield grains, which are essential now and will only be more so as the world population expands, rely on artificial fertilizer, pesticides, herbicides, farm machinery, and transportation to markets. All of these are derived from, or require, fossil fuel. Furthermore, we cannot count on maximizing food production for everyone in a society beset with hostilities and chaos. This situation will grow worse as time passes and stresses increase.

Greed

Greed for political power, money, land, water, and other natural resources creates a huge amount of human conflict and misery in the world today. On the personal level it creates inequality, leaving many powerless and impoverished. It disregards the needs of future generations that have no voice in what we do today, leaving their future to take care of itself on a depleted, overpopulated planet. Greed erupts at an international level as well, making it hard for nations to cooperate on issues like oceanic fish management and reducing carbon dioxide emissions. American politicians dare not tell their constituents to reduce their consumption or the people of emerging powers such as China, India, and Brazil that they cannot live like Americans do. Greed is making it hard for nations and states sharing a river to utilize it equitably. It's a strong force holding us on our current course toward a terrible future.

Inequality

Some people earn millions of dollars a year while many, especially in underdeveloped nations, do not have enough to eat, and lack schools, medical care, and clean water to drink. As the rich try to outdo each other by buying ever more extravagant yachts they rarely use, and purchasing gold and diamonds to show off, 15,000 children die every day of causes related to malnutrition.

In the United States the gap between the rich and poor has been widening as the graph in Figure 8 illustrates. If this continues we will become a very different kind of country than we were twenty years ago or are today. This could, when things get bad enough, end in revolution, as it has in the past in France, Russia, China, and elsewhere—if climate change does not overwhelm us first.

Many corporate executives, and their friends and admirers, see themselves as being the greatest benefits to society. The Walton family is certainly well

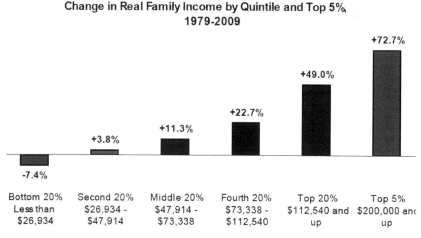

Figure 8. Historical income disparities. Source: U.S. Census Bureau

Figure 9. *Rising Sun,* a 450-foot yacht co-owned by Larry Ellison, CEO of the Oracle Corporation, and David Geffen, an American film producer. The yacht is equipped with jacuzzi bathrooms, gym and spa salons, a huge wine cellar, a private cinema with a giant plasma screen, and a basketball court on the main deck which also serves as a helicopter pad. Photo by Giorgio Ferretto.

Figure 10. Less fortunate Americans. Photo by Steve Liss/*americanpoverty.org*

rewarded and does provide many jobs. However, many more have been lost on "Main Street" when local businesses close, leaving vacant storefronts when a new Walmart opens up nearby.

Modern electronics and means of communication enable an ever smaller number of entertainers, musicians, businesses, and so forth to garner a large share of available opportunities, leaving others to languish. Most people accept this, making whomever or whatever is at the top their heroes, or favorite brands.

Dishonesty and corruption

Considerable damage is sustained and a huge amount of time, energy, and financial resources are consumed dealing with the consequences of lying, stealing, cheating, and corruption. The Internet has added new possibilities for criminals, often with anonymity and impunity. While most people are fairly honest, some individuals keep pushing and pushing, looking for opportunities for personal gain at the expense of others and society. Like an iceberg, most of what takes place here lies out of sight.

The temptation to "grease the wheels" is pervasive, even amongst reasonably honest people. In some societies, favors are an essential way of getting things done. When I spent time in China and India teaching urban planning, "favors" were taken for granted by virtually everyone. Sometimes American businesses trying to get contracts in foreign countries simply cannot get government business without making payoffs.

In the U.S. legislators are taken on golf outings and to expensive restaurants. Pharmaceutical companies entertain doctors and take them on vacations, etc., etc. Political contributions by lobbyists and many individuals and interest groups are simply payments to get something done a certain way. We rarely call this what it really is. Corruption appears to be the norm and it takes constant vigilance to keep it under control.

Misinformation

In order to avoid a crash while driving our car, we need accurate information about what is ahead of us out there. Likewise, we need correct information about our options in order to lead a safe, sensible life in this increasingly confusing, dangerous world—and we need to heed it. It is not always easy to get correct information. Charlatans mislead us to get our money. People with strong convictions, such as religious fundamentalists and conspiracy believers, try to convince us to accept their beliefs. Businesses work on our emotions to sell us things, may lie about the safety of their product, and occasionally fund organizations to mislead us, about climate change for example. Many politicians present messages that arouse primitive feelings such as fear and greed, and may try to convince us to vote against our own interests during political campaigns. Sources we choose for information may present information molded by the interests of their owners. Misinformation robs us of our basic human right to make a decision based on reality and our own interests, not someone else's.

We ourselves are responsible for much of our confusion. We are often guilty of accepting untruths because of our apathy, lack of curiosity, fuzzy thinking, and inclination to put a belief or agenda ahead of seeking and accepting evidence. Masses of people following bizarre goals or delusions make it extremely difficult for society to behave in a rational way. It seems that only a small minority of us place reality over religious or political agendas or beliefs. Basing action on these prevents us from dealing with the world as it is.

Intricacy and interaction

The issues today are so intertwined and complex, and so much is still unknown about the rapidly multiplying problems we face, that it is impossible to get an overall picture of what is taking place in the world today. While most of the problems we face appear manageable, when they interact and affect each other, it becomes clear that the consequences are considerably worse than the sum of the problems themselves. Ortega y Gasset, the Spanish liberal philosopher and essayist, warned us in 1930 when he wrote, "The disproportion between the complex subtlety of the problems and the minds that should study them will become greater if a remedy be not found, and it constitutes the basic tragedy of our civilization."[10] We have not recognized this yet.

IN SHORT

We are faced with two sets of problems that affect our well-being, those of the environment, and those embedded in our very nature, war for example. We are the root cause of both. We ignore these roots and go for the obvious, trying to deal with the consequences on superficial levels, problem by problem—and not very well. Standing back and objectively looking in from the outside, it is clear that our species is, slowly in our time, but rapidly in evolutionary time, bringing on its own demise. We are like passengers on a bus where most of us don't know or care where it is headed, but enjoy the ride and keep calling for more speed. The few who complain are labeled killjoys, "nuts," or alarmists and are ignored.

In order to grasp our situation today, it is essential to view it in a holistic way. I will try to paint a broad picture of what is making life difficult for people today and threatening the future of those to come. These things are well known, but when looked at as a whole rather than singly or in small groups, what they reveal is far more disturbing.

Part Two of this book is a concise, comprehensive survey of what is actually happening in the world today in nine essential areas. Unless you are up to date on all of these, you might find it helpful to read all, or selected sections, of Part Two before proceeding with the rest of Part One.

Chapter Four

WHAT COMES WITH BEING HUMAN

We go about our daily lives under illusions about what we really are. Many of us see ourselves as being very different from animals, but science tells us that basically we are not. Most likely nearly all of humanity's achievements, at first ignored or rejected by most people, were produced by relatively few individuals. Without such individuals, we would probably be living as we were 15,000 years ago. While we have amazing abilities and have made remarkable discoveries and inventions, we don't give adequate thought to the numerous ways we fall short of what we like to think we are.

OUR PRIMITIVE BRAIN

One cannot state our predicament more clearly than Edward O. Wilson did, "We have created a Star Wars civilization with Stone Age emotions, medieval institutions, and godlike technology."[11] Having powerful tools and weapons with hunting-gathering minds is the fundamental problem of our time.

Our brain's basic structure comes from early periods in evolution. Without wiping out its ties to a primitive past, it was added to and re-formed to meet the needs of ever higher forms of life, and over time that of a human hunting and gathering society. The result is a tradeoff between constraints imposed by its past, and the needs of that society. To achieve this, it utilizes a variety of remarkable techniques, which in turn, impose limitations on how we think. It is with these brains that we have developed the amazing complex civilization we now have. Unfortunately, we are not doing as good a job of managing it and it is now threatening our future. Our civilization has left our brains behind.

Our brains have served us well until recent centuries. In many ways they still do, however working as they always have, they are not attuned to the world as we have changed it, so they are getting us into trouble. Acting the way we once did in order to survive may now lead to our extinction. We need to understand why this is so. We will start by looking at an essential part of our neural system, a part without which a brain can do nothing at all, because it would know nothing of the world around itself.

Failings in our perception system

How we interact with our world depends on how we perceive it. Our view of reality is skewed by our place in it. I live among a very small percent of humanity that is extremely wealthy in a tiny fragment of time. This seems normal to me. I am an honest person and although I know better, I have an instinctive feeling that others think like I do. It takes vigilance on my part to fight this and avoid being taken advantage of. I have known a number of "operators" who do not trust anyone, and they lead their lives accordingly. Our different perspectives affect how we deal with the world around us and create misunderstandings and conflicts when we deal with each other.

Before, and during the period that life has existed on Earth, chemical and geological processes formed an environment that was relatively free of radiation and other things that are harmful to living cells. Toxins such as heavy metals were for the most part left in deposits or in stable compounds safely away from our food and water. Harmful ultraviolet light and cosmic rays were filtered by the atmosphere, but radiation necessary for photosynthesis was allowed to reach the earth's surface. The earth's atmosphere and life influenced each other to produce an environment that was safe and nourishing for life as we know it.

In the past we did not need to be aware of processes such as the carbon cycle, which is essential for all life on the planet. It was self-regulating and affected little by human activity. But today, we are changing its workings in dangerous ways by burning fossil fuels and reducing the earth's vegetation. It has taken us a long time to learn that we are also seriously reducing the number of species of both animals and plants on the planet. We do not feel our planet changing, and our responses to what is happening are halfhearted because we do not yet feel the consequences.

We are now living in an environment that is ever more rapidly going out of balance, but we have no natural mechanism that adequately alarms us about the dangers this entails. Our mental images of reality omit much of the data we need in order to understand this situation and deal with it safely.

Our minds can only notice change

Our perception system only responds to differences such as a change in color or intensity in our visual field, or a change in volume or pitch in sound. If there is no change, we notice nothing; if change is too gradual or too small, it will pass unnoticed.

In the past, people did not need to be aware of slow change such as increasing amounts of carbon dioxide in the atmosphere. Today it is essential that we notice the changes we are inflicting on the planet that will have significant impact on it over the years ahead. Like a frog in a pot of slowly heating water, unaware of the danger it is in until it is too late, few people notice the accumulating consequences of what we are doing. Often, because it makes us feel good, it is we who turn up the heat. We like what we do despite the damage we do not notice, so we keep doing it. We want more automobiles, fast food, and disposables. We like things as they are, with of course the constant introduction of still more "improvements"—which means still more consumption and waste with the consequences that accompany them.

We have grown so used to gradual change, that should it stop, we would be alarmed and worry. As noted earlier, we do not notice that day by day, the gradual changes, growing sprawl for example, we accept as normal and necessary to maintain our lifestyle are bringing about radical major changes that are damaging the biosphere and undermining our civilization.

Where we put our attention

A serious problem with many people today is that when they hear about climate change, or a prolonged drought in a distant country, they simply are not moved by such information. Our relative indifference to the environment beyond our immediate surroundings lies deep within us. The human brain evolved to commit itself emotionally to only a small piece of geography, and a limited band of kinsmen. Evolution shaped us to value what is close to us in time and space. That was essential for hunter-gatherers, as it could affect them and they could affect it. Edward O. Wilson put it this way. "For hundreds of millennia those who focused on short-term gains within a small circle of relatives and friends lived longer and left more offspring—even when their collective striving caused their chiefdoms and empires to crumble around them. The long view that might have saved their distant descendants required a vision and extended altruism instinctively difficult to marshal."[12] Today our actions affect, and we are affected by, things thousands of miles away from us and far into the future, however they interest most of us little.

Our visual sense of perspective makes an object that is far from us appear smaller than it would appear if it were close. An automobile bearing down on me is very real and needs my attention, whereas one that is two miles away does not. Nevertheless, the intensity of our perception of something is not necessarily in direct proportion to the importance of the thing itself. This kind of thinking is far more serious when applied to catastrophes like climate change that are certain to happen in the not too distant future.

We now live in a milieu where our feelings about an event can be totally unrelated to its importance or to our actual involvement with it. Many of us are unmoved or even pleased when the U.S. government cuts foreign aid that among other things has been used to feed malnourished children. A story can touch us where facts cannot. We are much more moved when a cute pet dog is hit by a car in a TV drama than when an announcer tells us that 15,000 children are facing starvation in another part of the world. This, of course, is normal human behavior—the pet dog, real or fictional, appears near and real to us; children in faraway places do not. We can be very moved by the unimportant things that are right around us right now, and hardly moved at all by huge things such as what's happening to our planet over time. From what I see observing those around me, in their minds the rest of the people on the planet don't exist. This kind of thinking is getting us into deep trouble in an interconnected, overpopulated, unsustainable world, where things that we are doing every day may affect all of us profoundly before long. The state of the economy appears more important to us than issues involving global survival, which we cannot feel. Today, we must often make decisions about such situations—without having the mental equipment to evaluate their true importance to us.

Our interests

Our foraging ancestors focused their interest on their sources of food, surroundings, family, neighbors, the weather, etc.—things directly connected to their needs and welfare. Some of our interests today are directed to the well-being of ourselves and our families, however a larger number of them now have nothing or little to do with the survival of ourselves or our species. Our attention today is consumed by huge amounts of information about sports, entertainment, and trivia, and information about products provided to us by constant advertising. Few of us show real interest in things affecting the future or our environment.

Our sense of time

We have a poor comprehension of time, or interest in it beyond our own life span. We do not feel how our life today fits into our species history since 1850, when there were less than eighteen percent as many people living on the planet, let alone since *Homo sapiens* began its climb to our current civilization with the development of agriculture. Our grasp of time is best when measured in minutes or hours. As periods become much shorter or longer, we have increasing difficulty relating to and comprehending them. We evolved to think in terms of one three generations away, at most. As E.O. Wilson pointed out above, looking farther ahead or further afield would have distracted early humans and hunter-gatherers from what was essential for them. We are now living in an environment that is ever more rapidly going out of balance, but we have no natural mechanism that adequately alarms us to this and the dangers it entails. Individuals pursuing short-term goals, often involving money or power, have an easier time achieving them than people with long-term goals. This puts them in a better position to move forward, and over time tends to perpetuate itself and build up.

The factors above may well explain why few people show much interest in the future further than the next two, five, or maybe ten or twenty years. Science fiction has its enthusiasts, but has little to do with reality. Some people have longer-term interests in aspects of the future such as in medicine, aviation, communications, weaponry, education, or their retirement, for example, and as it relates to their profession. However, only a few have more than a cursory interest in the whole, such as what our lives and our planet will be like twenty or fifty years from now. This lack of interest and concern leaves our planet and future generations with few protectors in this dangerous time.

While we often plan for the very near future, even governments and organizations generally ignore what might happen more than five years ahead. A large and well-known hospital in Chicago I did master planning for had made its last set of additions as if there never would be more growth. Not much later this made expansion very awkward and expensive. A retirement community I know spent a million dollars building a garden for its residents, and several years later they destroyed it to make room for more assisted living facilities. It is hard for many of us to understand that in a few years things can be different than they are right now. We have all heard complaints about "those welfare recipients who spend their money as soon as they get it." Are we any better than they are, especially when the consequences of our own neglect are far graver?

Our overrated ability to reason

The growing complexity of our world today requires clear thinking far beyond what was ever needed before. We need to see connections between things and events, both in the present and over time, however we often fail to notice and deal with the most obvious, such as the need for Egypt, historically a food exporter, to now import large quantities of food as a result of its rapid population growth. The gap between the need for rational thinking and reality keeps growing and so do the demands on leaders from an ignorant public that thinks mainly in the short term. There is no organized effort to counter this problem in a holistic way.

We have self-flattering illusions about our ability to reason. For example, when we get in an argument over some idea, both sides are usually convinced that they are right, but they can't be. If we were honest and clearheaded, arguments would be quickly settled, and both sides would be grateful for becoming wiser. There would be no argument over climate change, and the world's people would settle on one idea of God. There still would be conflicts over political and economic systems as values come into play, nevertheless reason would eliminate faulty notions such as the possibility of unlimited growth in a finite space.

Our brains evolved to help us survive as hunter-gatherers. In that lifestyle, there was a limited need for rational thought—in fact when quick decisions were needed, spending time thinking things out could be dangerous. Consequently even today we gravitate toward quick, easily understood solutions. Our brain was very well suited for the needs of that time, however given the complexities of the world we now live in, and its dangers, it leaves us ill-prepared to deal with them. We have not learned how to restrain the powerful impact we are having on our planet.

Irrationality exists worldwide, involving most people, governments, and the media. Skimping on worthwhile and essential projects, nations spend huge amounts of money on armaments and hostilities. When we look at all the misery and costs of war it makes no sense not to have eliminated it, but we haven't. The automobile, air conditioning, and ever higher standards of living are irresponsibly promoted around the world as the burning of diminishing supplies of fossil fuels adds ever more carbon dioxide and particulates to the atmosphere.

How we do think

Evolution found a system of thinking for us that largely circumvents the need for logic. Our everyday thinking most often bypasses logic and depends to a large extent on referring back to what we know, on the way our knowledge is organized in memory, and on how such knowledge is evoked. I observe this in myself. If I want to go from A to B as I have a number of times before, I do not analyze my route for efficiency and pleasantness, I just go the way I have before. When I meet someone I don't know, in order to be able to interact with him quickly, I rely on stereotypes my mind has previously constructed. My subconscious guides me. Unfortunately, this way of thinking can leave important gaps in the way we deal with reality.

What we already know and our biases largely determine the information we use in our thinking processes. Many people have a great attraction to ideas that have no grounding in fact, that are based on superstition, biases, and political or religious agendas. We therefore make many important decisions on partial or faulty information, which when depending on association rather than logic for decisions, can easily produce erroneous conclusions. These erroneous conclusions become new knowledge and in turn distort new data selection and thought processes. This can open the door to trouble when dealing with reality, which includes complex problems such as those involving politics, international relations, economics, and environmental systems.

This failure extends far beyond individuals; it includes the media, educators, and governments. This leaves us ignorant of where geometric population and economic growth are taking us, for example. Few people give thought to or comprehend the consequences of exponential growth. If one starts with an empty bucket, adds one drop of water and every day doubles the amount added to the bucket, change seems very slow at first. Nevertheless, in time the bucket becomes half-full and the next day is full, and then the following day a full bucket's worth spills over. This lack of understanding is now taking us into very dangerous territory.

Need for and effect of emotion

Emotions play an extremely important part in our lives. They arouse us to act, most importantly when we need to take action. Nevertheless, on their own they can mislead us. They have a far greater power over us than evidence or statistics. The fact that we are more moved when a fictional dog is hit by a car, as I mentioned earlier, than by statistics about starving children on the other side of the world reveals a way of thinking that is getting us into trouble.

Emotions are needed to persuade a public to meet challenges where sacrifice is required. However, they can mislead on a grand scale as Hitler did in his hate-arousing speeches during the Third Reich.

Clear thinking does not come easy

Clear thinking does not come easy for us, and we make little effort to do better. For example, we have trouble balancing risks. Some suburbanites do not hesitate to jump into their automobile without fastening their seat belts, and as they talk on their cell phones spend several hours every day driving along busy freeways listening to broadcasts reporting current accidents on those very freeways. Some of these people are afraid to visit "downtown" even when statistics tell them that it is safe. They do not see that the real danger is in getting there.

Irrationality erupts in many ways on an international level. In October 1988 the United States, the Soviet Union, and 150 journalists spent $5,795,000 to cover the story of three grey whales caught in a rapidly closing hole in the Arctic ice. During this event people around the world empathized with the whales and followed the situation on television daily as it unfolded. Unnoticed, during the same three-week period the world population increased by nearly 5,000,000 people and half a million children died as a result of malnutrition. And ironically during an average three-week period in 1987, approximately 600 whales were commercially slaughtered with with little public outcry.

Although many things remain a mystery, science has given us insights that help us better understand the universe, our planet, and ourselves. Nonetheless, in spite of considerable evidence, many people are not satisfied with, or are even perturbed by scientific findings. The popularity of astrology, fraudulent gurus, pseudoscience, and conspiracy theories attest to this. Many individuals and powerful leaders refuse to consider scientific evidence. We just cannot believe that the kind of world evidence shows we are headed for can actually come about. Special interests have taken advantage of and promoted this confusion for their own benefit. Rational public discussion of topics such as birth control and climate change becomes impossible. Information can produce anxiety, so people may react with denial, or with blind faith that their leaders or technology and business will deal with the problem without requiring them to make sacrifices.

The right to family planning and abortion is under continual debate. There is little real discussion beyond the "right to lifers" shouting that abortion is murder, and the pro-choice people shouting that women should have the right to choose. There is little objective debate about when a human life begins, or what kind of a life unwanted children will lead and what their impact on society will be.

In order to get the economy growing, which they insist is essential, Republicans repeatedly say we must keep taxes down for the rich in order to enable them to create jobs. They are not publicly challenged to explain how that works when huge numbers of people are put out of work to save money instead of eliminating tax loopholes and raising taxes on people rapidly growing richer. A high percentage of political campaigning consists of repeating, repeating, and repeating slogans. Most public issues are dealt with by appealing to our most primitive instincts with little honest backup data and rational thought, and the public accepts it that way.

Consequences of fuzzy thinking. We often find ourselves in positions we cannot tolerate, where what we see challenges our wishes, beliefs we hold dear, and our way of life. A trait psychologists call "motivated reasoning" impels us to cling to erroneous beliefs in spite of overwhelming evidence against them. Instead of objectively searching for accurate information that either confirms or dispels a particular belief, we tend to seek out information, true or false, that confirms what we already believe. This way of thinking is widespread and has a devastating effect on how we live on this planet. People who see climate change as threatening their way of life or their income embrace ideas and individuals who deny that humanity has any effect on it, or that eating beef contributes to it.

Ignoring or distorting our view of reality becomes more dangerous as our impact on the planet increases and our world becomes more complex. Our attraction to quick, easy, simplistic solutions to complex problems, and failure to think about their side effects, is pervasive. For example, many people think we do not need to concern ourselves with environmental problems. "Nature, God, and human ingenuity have always taken care of us and will again." Looking at evidence and a little clear thinking would show that by counting on this, we are entrusting our future to hope rather than evidence. It should be clear to us that while we have removed constraints on our ecological niche, we have not assumed responsibility for restoring stability.

It would seem that our inability to think logically would disturb us, and that we would work hard to overcome it. For most of us, this is not the case. In fact we do a poor job of using the limited abilities we have, and we are quite satisfied to let it go at that.

Imagination

There are two ways we learn about the world beyond ourselves. Sensation, which tells us what is happening to or right around ourselves, is far stronger than intellectual perception, which tells us what is happening beyond ourselves. What we see and feel is stronger than what we learn secondhand from outside sources. The more imaginative we are, the better we are able to narrow this gap between sensation and perception and gain a broader view of reality.

Imagination plays an important part in civil society. It allows us to empathize with other people. It allows us to picture people in far-off places or in the future. Imagination helps us to visualize different possible futures and to construct "what if" scenarios. It prompts us to extend our concern beyond ourselves. Today, individuals, organizations, and governments are regularly confronted with situations that may extend further beyond our immediate surroundings and time than we ever had to concern ourselves with before. What we do today affects others we cannot see.

Imagination varies greatly from person to person, but on the average, it is weak. While this was suitable for the needs of our simple past, it is far from adequate for the needs of today. Unfortunately, people who occupy positions of power are likely to have especially weak imaginations. For this reason many people see them as "sound, practical people" who can be trusted. Too often such individuals ascribe poverty to laziness, environmental concerns to extremism, and can enter a war with little empathy for the victims, or objective vision of its possible outcome.

Evidence and statistics indicate that in a few decades our world will be very different than it is today, yet it is very hard for most of us us to grasp that simple fact. It takes imagination to picture a future unlike the present. Global warming and future food and water shortages do not arouse people the way a recession or tax increase does. Problems close at hand or similar to those we have already experienced are easy to comprehend; others are not. We see our current environment and wasteful lifestyle as being normal. Not sensing that there are starving people on this planet, for us it seems normal to drive between five to twenty miles to a shopping center and to vacation at a luxurious resort in the Caribbean.

COMPELLING PRIMARY DRIVES

Evolution's influence

Instinctive drives that served our forefathers well are sometimes grossly inappropriate in the physical and social environment of the twenty-first century. The oldest and most primitive parts of our brain, which we share with frogs and lizards, are close to the spinal column. They control the instincts, drives, and emotions needed for us to act, and for the survival of our species. Hunger impels us to eat when we need food, the sex drive causes us to procreate, and fear initiates our defensive or offensive mechanisms. Higher-level motivators promote kindness, cooperation, and peace, as well as selfishness, jealousy, our attraction to violence, and our drive for status.

Fear has a great influence on us. It can protect us from many dangers, but it can also paralyze us or lead us in dangerous directions. Fear of failure can stop us from doing good things. Once aroused, fear can start a chain of irrational thoughts and strong emotions. It can begin a cycle of suspicion and hostility leading to violence and can put us at the mercy of charlatans and despots. Jealousy and excessive ambition warp our thinking and undermine the cooperation that is necessary for groups to function constructively. Vanity clouds our perception of reality and often prevents us from recognizing and solving serious problems. Selfishness and greed for money and/or power, which once just helped individuals survive and pass on their genes, can today divide a society into a few living in extreme luxury, while others starve, and lack education and medical attention. Together with our tendency toward violence, these primal drives make it difficult for those promoting cooperation and peace, and can lead to war and huge amounts of human misery and suffering.

Competitiveness

Evolution favors winners. During our evolution people who successfully contended for food, shelter, mates, and other advantages produced more descendants than others. Competitiveness was thus strengthened and became an intrinsic trait of our species. We reinforce this quality today by further rewarding those who successfully compete with money, respect, and fame. Highly skilled athletes, business tycoons, war heroes, and even dictators, such as Napoleon, are respected and admired. Many of us value success more than personal qualities such as kindness, honesty, knowledge, and wisdom. Consequently, our society is highly competitive.

This competitiveness spills into arguments and discussions where we are usually more interested in winning than in coming to a rational conclusion or in learning something new. Arguments often end up as shouting matches, each side trying to convince the other, without hearing what the other side has to say. Most of us really are not all that interested in truth; we like to win. We see our personal prestige as hanging on it.

While worldwide cooperation is now essential for resolving environmental problems, our drive to come out on top makes cooperation difficult. Most people and governments focus their concerns on their own nation and feel that going beyond that is sacrificing their national sovereignty. People do not reward their leaders for international cooperation. The refusal of nations to collaborate has led to massive overfishing and our inability to effectively deal with climate change.

Violence

We cannot say that the Germans, the Japanese, the Serbs, or the Hutus are worse than the rest of us. Our basic makeup is the same as theirs. I see violence in myself. Although I was generally a peaceful child, at times I did cruel things like shooting at birds with a BB gun for fun, stepping on

Figure 11. "The Hanging," by Jacques Callot, 1592–1635. Wellcome Library, London/Creative Commons

ants, and pulling the wings off flies. Today, when I hear of gross injustice or torture, images of revenge on the perpetrators come up in my mind. Fortunately, civilizing forces work on me, and my own sense of decency constrains such urges. Until we stop pointing our fingers at others, and recognize the potential for violence in ourselves, and address it, we will continue to perpetrate acts of brutality in the guise of doing good.

The capacity for violence appears in many species from insects to our own. In our case it is organized society that has kept it under control. David Anderson, Howard Hughes Medical Investigator, put it this way on a television program.[13] "We have these inborn tendencies to aggression that are hardwired into brain areas like the hypothalamus and the amygdala, but we learn through parenting and training to keep these in check and that is due to the...prefrontal cortex that exerts this conscious control to suppress aggressive impulses."

There is a strong inclination in human nature for the strong to take advantage of of people in a weaker position than themselves, to maltreat the elderly, children, and employees, and for men to brutalize women, etc. Anthony Storr, the noted English psychiatrist, wrote, "It is clear that human beings possess a marked hereditary predisposition toward aggressive behavior which they share with other animals and which serves a number of positive functions. An animal has to be able to compete for whatever resources of food are available. Sexual selection is ensured by competition for mates.... Animals which live in groups tend to establish hierarchies which reduce conflict between individuals...."[14] Here too, we have evolved to meet the needs for individuals to thrive in foraging societies.

While it sometimes seemed that certain people were peaceful, such as the Mayans and the Pygmies, when more was learned about them, we found they were not. We are not unlike one of our closest relatives with whom we share ninety-eight percent of our genes. Jane Goodall discovered that chimpanzees, once thought of as peaceful, make vicious attacks on neighboring groups. Our tendency to violence lies deep within us.

The desire for revenge, when we feel we have been wronged, was responsible for much violence in the past and still is. The Bible is passionate about revenge, giving us expressions like "an eye for an eye," and "vengeance is mine." The subject of revenge has fostered great literary works, such as *Hamlet*, and it takes an important place in many tribal and modern societies today, adding to the difficulties of maintaining peace.

Every day the news media are filled with stories about conflict and violence. News about constructive actions generally has to move over for stories about competition and brutality. Journalists, politicians, businesspeople, and in fact most people focus their attention on money, "success," competition, and power, rather than on cooperation, creating, nurturing, justice, and truth. We seem to be fascinated with conflict and ferocity.

Figure 12. The Arc de Triomphe in Paris, erected to honor those who fought for France during the Napoleonic Wars. Library of Congress

Figure 13. Sawing of three homosexuals, from a fifteenth-century print. This is a slow, painful means of execution, since as long as the brain is supplied with blood and oxygen, the victim does not die until the saw reaches the heart or lungs. Wikimedia Commons

While there are a few sociopaths without conscience out there, our inclination to violent behavior in various ways is widespread.

In 1914, the English poet Julian Grenfell wrote his mother, "I've never been so fit or nearly so happy in my life before: I adore the fighting and the continual interest which compensates for every disadvantage....I adore war; it is like a big picnic without the objectlessness of a picnic."[15] Seven months later, he was wounded and died.

Gustave Le Bon, the nineteenth/twentieth century French psychologist and sociologist, noted, "among the most savage members of the French Convention were to be found inoffensive citizens who, under ordinary circumstances, would have been peaceful notaries or virtuous magistrates."[16]

A famous controlled experiment conducted by Philip Zimbardo and his colleagues at Stanford University revealed cruelty in normal, healthy U.S. male college students.[17] A group of twenty-four were randomly divided into groups of "prisoners" and "guards." Suitable cells and uniforms were provided and the experiment was to last two weeks. Within a short time the "guards" appeared to derive pleasure from insulting, threatening, and dehumanizing the "prisoners" who became depressed, anxious, passive, and self-deprecating. These feelings became so intense that the experiment was terminated after six days. Most distressing to the researchers was the facility with which "normal" young men could adopt sadistic behavior.

New York Times correspondent Nicholas Kristof came across secret Communist Party documents that attest to large-scale cannibalism in the

Guangxi region of southern China during the Cultural Revolution. He describes one incident. "The first person to strip meat from the body of one school principal was the former girlfriend of the man's son; she wanted to show she had no sympathy for him and was just as 'red' as anybody else. At some high schools, students butchered and roasted their teachers and principals in the school courtyard and feasted on the meat to celebrate triumph over 'counterrevolutionaries.' "[18]

While we normally contain ourselves, it seems there is no end to the brutality we are capable of. As I have noted, Steven Pinker has demonstrated that the world today is far less violent than it was in our past. Still, we are the same people and should governments and social structures with their constraints break down, the worst in us can break out. In the past executions were not just a punishment for misdeeds, but were used to inflict as much pain as possible on criminals. As Christians know the Romans used crucifixion as a means of execution. Spikes were often driven through hands and feet to hold the prisoner on the cross, where over hours or a few days he would die in terrible pain. During the Middle Ages, breaking on the wheel, the iron maiden, immersion in freezing water, exposure to hungry rats, dismemberment, drawing and quartering, and sawing were used to inflict terrible pain during execution.

Avarice

People have a variety of interests that drive them to fit into society in different ways. Some just want to get by and will fit in wherever they can. Others have strong interests that steer them toward, for example: teaching, science, the military, working with people, public service, preparing food, engineering, business, art, or taking care of the sick or victims of a natural disaster. For some the smell of money or power draws them to do whatever will help them get it, and there are some who just want to win, to come out on top and beat the other guy. Often the most aggressive, competitive, confrontational people are like this. Some of them reach their goal, and because of their money and/or power become weighty players in society. Some of these people achieve positions in occupations that make or sell a useful product, others in something harmful like producing cancer-causing cigarettes or fast foods leading to many early deaths due to obesity and diabetes. Others engage outright in criminal activities like producing drugs. To gain political power, some people will sell themselves for campaign contributions. That is about as corrupt as it can get.

In the United States the CEOs of corporations that do harmful things such as making soft drinks and promoting them in schools are paid multiples of what teachers, scientists, and even Nobel Laureates get. Why are they not seen for what they are, individuals who harm others to make money? To me this sounds like murder, yet many people admire them for their money and position, while they give little esteem to those who collect their trash, a most useful and essential occupation.

Reaching a position with economic or political power becomes a positive feedback loop because it brings on more money and power. The person doing work he enjoys or does for the public good does not improve his position in the "game," and is left in a weaker position compared with those pursuing money or power. Those at the bottom build up debt, fall still further behind, and are forgotten.

When I first saw the palace of Versailles with its lavish halls and gardens it became clear to me that there are no limits to what some human beings want. In our time, the skyrocketing compensation and perks demanded by corporate executives bears this out.

Isolation and arrogance of the wealthy

Several times when I was in grammar school I found myself being driven around by a chauffeur in an expensive car. I must confess it made me feel special, better than those other people I saw out there on the streets. The very rich do not feel the pain of the poor. They separate themselves from the rest of us and confine their personal relationships to one another—the rest of us just don't count. With their clubs, private schools, private jets, exclusive vacation spots, and all the rest, the wealthy stick with those who share their interests, concerns, and lifestyle. Their interests are largely money itself, the means for acquiring it, how to spend it, other wealthy people, and political support for their values. Their success in gaining power and money gives them self-assuredness, arrogance, and the expectation that others should kowtow to them. Because of their financial success, many of them are convinced that they themselves have the best understanding of the "real world," and they ignore much of the knowledge and wisdom of those who know more, including what scientists say. Few scientists are rich, so they are not taken seriously.

Those at the top often smugly take pride in humanity's achievements, particularly by individuals like themselves, overlooking the fact that nearly all inventions and new ideas, as noted earlier, were the achievements

Figure 14. Fairfield Pond in the Hamptons is the home of billionaire Ira Rennert. This home, valued at $170-200 million, has twenty-nine bedrooms, thirty-nine bathrooms, a basketball court, two tennis courts, a bowling alley, and a $150,000 hot tub. Wikimedia Commons

Figure 15. A homeless woman sits on a street in Chicago. Photo © Peer Grimm/dpa/Corbis

of relatively few individuals. Left to tribal chieftains and CEO types, we would probably be living much as we were 15,000 years ago, with some of us hoarding more seashells and amber than others. These limited people with their money, power, and contacts have an influence on the rest of us and the world far beyond their numbers.

Their morals. Occasionally I receive a flyer in the mail from 20/20/20, a WonderWork charity program, telling me that one million of the blind children around the world could have their eyesight restored through a $300 surgery. I find it hard to understand how some people can enjoy staying in a hotel room that costs $1,000 a night or more while many children are left to lead a life of darkness, and others grow up mentally retarded for lack of an adequate diet as children.

The affluent love their money, and do not part with it easily. I have a friend who is a doctor and had an uncle who owned an art gallery. Both complained that the hardest people to collect from are those with a lot of money. Studies bear this out. According to a *Chronicle of Philanthropy* study, "middle-class Americans give a far bigger share of their discretionary income to charities than the wealthy. Households that earn $50,000 to $75,000 give an average of 7.6 percent of their discretionary income to charity, compared with an average of 4.2 percent for people who make $100,000 or more."[19] The love of money drives some rich people well beyond stinginess. In a study on honesty at UC Berkeley researchers consistently found that upper-class participants in experiments were more likely than other people to lie and cheat when gambling or negotiating; cut people off when driving, and endorse unethical behavior in the workplace.[20] A friend of mine who worked in a university bookstore told me that law and business students were the ones to watch.

Vincent Teresa, convicted mobster turned informer, speaking of his dealings with "legitimate" businesspeople said: "People are greedy, especially businesspeople, and if there is a way to make a fast buck, they'll grab it." When he was selling stolen goods to discount houses, for example: "The discount store owners were greedier than the mob. They'd buy all you could get them, no questions asked, whether it was men's and women's clothing, furs, television sets, appliances, or shoes. I could have sold them ten trailer loads of goods a day if I'd had them available, particularly around the Christmas holidays."[21]

Some money or power seeking individuals go further. They are highly intelligent sociopaths who will resort to any means to achieve their ends. In business, Kenneth Lay, "Bernie" Ebbers, and "Bernie" Madoff come to mind, and in politics Hitler, Stalin, Idi Amin, and Saddam Hussein.

BELIEFS

The human need for beliefs

Beliefs are essential for us to effectively interact with the world and with each other. We must believe that the sun will come up and our bank will still be in business tomorrow. For society to function well and effectively, we should be able to believe each other, although too often we can't. Our inner models of the world around us would be very incomplete if they relied only on what we could observe. The earth would probably be flat for us if we did not believe what others told us. History would be a blank—and so would science, unless we had conducted the research ourselves. No society can function without beliefs, and where it lacks them will manufacture them.

Nearly all of us want simple, satisfying explanations for what is happening to and around us. For some, not knowing is terrifying. Without explanations for significant events, we lack a consistent foundation for our behavior. To satisfy this rudimentary need, we believe and accept many things as being true with or without evidence that can justify our doing so. A belief is rarely a conclusion reached after an honest intellectual search. It bothers few of us that the world's people hold widely differing and often conflicting religious beliefs, for example, and thus most, if not all, of them must be wrong.

When we cannot observe a link between data, our desire for an explanation compels us to invent a fictitious one, bizarre as it may be. This has often led to serious trouble, and it still does. In his book *The Improbable Machine: What the New Upheaval in Artificial Intelligence Research Reveals About How the Mind Really Works*, Jeremy Campbell noted, "We can turn nonsense into sense because that is the way the brain has been designed for a world where a fast, plausible interpretation is often better than a slow, certain one."[22]

Although we often lack the curiosity, or don't want to make the effort to look at the facts, we tenaciously hold onto unfounded beliefs, and let them guide our lives. We "know" when we often really don't.

Two thousand years ago, Julius Caesar wrote, "Men willingly believe what they wish." What they wish might be what their peers or charismatic leaders proclaim, what they were brought up to believe by their parents or an institution, whatever provides easy answers, or simply fills their emotional needs. Our minds are influenced by our political and religious agendas and the groups we belong to. It matters a lot to us to have a belief that fits in with our group—holding a position that is at odds with our peers on a controversial subject can make life difficult. Consequently, it makes sense for people to pay attention to "getting it right" relative to their peers. Just as birds of a feather flock together, people usually prefer the company of those whose belief systems do not greatly differ from their own. This reduces social friction and cognitive dissonance. However, it also minimizes people's opportunity to examine new and contrary information that might lead to reassessment of their beliefs, and widen their outlook.

When times are stressful, people look for security and answers, and are vulnerable to demagogues with simplistic answers to their problems. They are also likely to blame groups and individuals different than themselves. They can then become fodder for fanatical groups like the Nazis or extreme religious groups such as some Christian fundamentalists or extreme Wahhabi Muslims, for example.

We have a strong force within us that tells us that what we believe is right and rational. Few people question their religious beliefs or their social and political convictions even though most of the world's people think differently from one another. This stubbornness prevents us from questioning, thinking, and delving into a reality we shut ourselves off from. Worse, it erects barriers between people, prevents them from cooperating, and too often leads to bloodshed.

Beliefs can make us ignore facts

We can arrive at beliefs in at least two ways. One, by evaluating verifiable information, the other, by finding things that support our point of view or agenda and make us feel good. Fallacious beliefs can be dangerous. Many people see science like a religion, as a matter of belief. Disregarding evidence, a sizeable percentage of Americans simply don't believe in evolution or that humans contribute to climate change.

Religious and political agendas have a powerful influence over us and often preempt reality. Psychologist Leon Festinger had this to say, "...A man with a conviction is a hard man to change. Tell him you disagree and he turns away. Show him facts or figures and he questions your sources. Appeal to logic and he fails to see your point."[24] Psychiatrist Anthony Storr wrote, "...A dogma is suspect; and it seems to me that most of the harm in the world is done by those who are dogmatically certain that they are right. For being absolutely right means that those who disagree are

absolutely wrong. Those who are absolutely wrong are of course dangerous to society and must be eliminated."[25]

Bizarre beliefs can affect large segments of society. Again, Anthony Storr:
"We may imagine that so-called normal people could never believe in anything so ludicrous as the delusional systems of the insane, yet historical evidence suggests the opposite. Whole societies have been persuaded without
much difficulty to accept the most absurd calumnies about minority groups
portrayed as enemies of the majority."[26]

Many people recognize that there are environmental problems, however they believe that we can manage to live with fifteen billion people on
the planet, and that everyone will be well fed and we will all be living better. Even if they accept that global warming is on its way, they believe that
measures such as building floodwalls along coastal areas will solve the
problem without requiring them to reduce their energy usage or change
their lifestyle. When the effects of global warming become widespread
and food and water supplies become critical, many individuals simplisti-
cally believe that we will be able to quickly turn things around. We have
always managed to overcome problems in the past, and we will continue
to do so. Some religious believers will say that these hardships are God's
will, and we should accept them.

The consequences of apathy

When people are confronted with information on something of importance that they can affect, some will be stirred up and respond as best they
can, some will be informed, but do little or nothing, and others will be unmoved and do nothing. In 1941 it took the bombing of Pearl Harbor to
awaken Americans to the dangers they were facing. Our county virtually
turned on a dime and set out to fight the Axis. Today, serious environmental threats are here, but because they do not happen suddenly, they arouse
few people. Nor do they affect all people equally—the wealthy and decision-makers who could take action are affected the least and last. Meanwhile, the media continue to focus on issues like the economy, politics, and
disasters such as floods and earthquakes, which they see as important, and
politicians are more interested in protecting their jobs. As long as this is the
case, apathy will reign and it will be hard to take the actions now needed to
contain or prevent inevitable consequences. Most people do not respond to
things until they have already happened or are right in front of us. As they
say, we don't lock the barn door until the horses have been stolen.

Chapter Five

OUR MODERN SOCIETY

THE PSYCHOLOGY OF SOCIETY

Working together should enable us to resolve a broad range of problems better than single individuals can, but sadly, we know this often is not so. When people work together more knowledge, more talent, and more ideas are available, however complicating factors such as groupthink, bureaucracy, individual stubbornness, greed, jealousy, destructive competition, and status seeking come into play. Rational, responsible behavior becomes even more difficult, and when we attempt to work together on a large scale as in a democratic government, decisions can be hard to reach or even be perverted.

Some years ago I attended a weekend workshop run by a sociologist friend. At the start the attendees were divided into groups and told to organize ourselves, and that later we would interact with the other organized groups. With much ado and jockeying for power, we elected officers and created positions for those left over in our group. I wanted to discuss the purpose and goals of our organization, but in the scramble this aroused no interest whatsoever. Near the end of the weekend, we were told that we would soon start interacting with the other groups. Immediately our discussion turned to how we could protect ourselves and get the better of the other groups. My friend had never suggested that conflict or competition was a goal for these interactions—this behavior just sprang up from deep within us. We were not interested in the purpose of our interaction; we just wanted to prevail over the other groups.

Such behavior is well known to social psychologists. In 1954 Muzafer Sherif conducted his famous two-week Robber's Cave experiment. Twenty-two psychologically normal eleven- and twelve-year-old boys were brought to a summer camp setting where they were split into two groups. In the first phase of the experiment members of each group got to know each other, social norms developed, leadership structure emerged, and the boys developed an attachment to their own groups. In the second phase the groups were ask to compete in a series of contests; and then conflicts emerged, including the raiding of each other's cabins. In the third phase the groups were brought together and given tasks where they had to cooperate. When the experiment was drawing to a close the boys were asked to describe the characteristics of each group. They rated their own group favorably and the others unfavorably. In William Golding's book, *Lord of the Flies*, which later became a movie, such behavior got far out of hand. Reading history or listening to the news today reveals far worse about how human groups can interact with each other.

Groupthink

Belonging to groups that share our values, beliefs, and agendas offers security. Independent thinking can get us in trouble, so it's easiest to keep our thoughts in line with those around us. For most people getting along and joining the crowd rewards us with friends and is the easiest way to get through life. Conformity, however, can get us caught up in the hysteria of a crowd at a football game, or far worse.

For various reasons some individuals are drawn to fanatical groups with beliefs that lead them to separate from and at times even take strong action against those outside. Currently young Talibans are willing to sacrifice their lives to kill "infidels." Charismatics can overpower rational thinking in many people. On November 18 of 1978, 918 people died in Jonestown, Guyana, most of them taking their own lives following the directions of their leader Reverend James Warren "Jim" Jones. There are many other incidents of strange behavior by members of groups.

Bizarre behavior can affect whole nations, and their citizens. In the young democracy of the United States people like Thomas Jefferson felt it was proper for some people to own other people. Those feelings pervaded much of the world of that time. Later, Germany, one of the most educated, cultured nations in the early twentieth century, turned into one of the worst under the Nazis.

When individuals belong to a group they can easily do things they normally would abhor. Christopher R. Browning, professor of history at Pacific Lutheran University, studied a battalion of middle-aged, lower-middle-class

Figure 16. The Jonestown massacre, November 18, 1978, in which 918 people died. Photo by David Hume, Kennerly/Getty

Figure 17. Germans giving a Nazi salute, with August Landmesser, who was married to a Jewish woman, refusing to do so. He paid for that. Wikimedia Commons

family men, reserve policemen from Hamburg, Germany, who had recently been drafted and brought to Poland in 1942. Few were racial fanatics or Nazis. On July 13 of that year, in the Polish village Józefów, they rounded up the Jews, selected several hundred as "work Jews," and shot the rest. They were not forced to do this but were given the chance to refuse. Twelve of the 500 did; the rest participated to varying degrees. During the sixteen months following this massacre, they participated in the shooting of 38,000 Jews and the deportation of 45,000. After conducting many interviews years later, Browning concluded that the reason so few refused to participate had to do with career ambition and peer pressure. They did not want to lose face in front of their comrades.[27] As David Anderson, Howard Hughes Medical Investigator, put it, "What happens in genocide is that it becomes socially acceptable for one group to do terrible things to another group."[28]

What this says when put together with what we know about ordinary businesspeople promoting harmful products for profit, and scientists willing to develop terrible weapons for tyrants, does not speak well for humanity. It demonstrates that large numbers of people are willing to do almost anything if it is condoned by their peers. This is what we are like, fortunately with many individual exceptions. We do in fact have the ability to control our primitive drives.

Society too ignores

In order to live sustainably, we must deal with reality as it exists, not with some fantasy of our mind we might prefer. Although tradition is a stabilizing force in society, it often supersedes good sense. Time moves on and we will be in trouble if we do not recognize and safely manage what we face today. One would think that intelligent, reasonable people and governments would, but all too often they do not.

There is plenty of evidence to show us that we are headed towards a more crowded world beset with shortages of food and water. A little thought will reveal that the future will be far worse as population continues to grow, topsoils erode, and fish catches decline further. Yet scientists and publicly available data are ignored. Instead, most of us choose to listen to people who tell us what we would like to hear. Many influential political and religious leaders cast aside what scientists tell us about the consequences of unending population growth, the impending depletion of natural resources, global warming, etc., and ignore the steps needed to mitigate these threats.

Creationists, determined to keep evolution out of textbooks, have a devastating effect on teaching rational thinking to young people. More than occasionally I hear recognized "energy experts" and economists discussing the future of fossil fuels as if they will never run out. They talk about it as if the problem of climate change did not exist, totally ignoring what the vast majority of climate scientists tell us, and James Hansen's warning about the coming Venus syndrome should we consume all our fossil fuel reserves. Global warming and other environmental problems were rarely discussed in the 2012 U.S. presidential campaign.

Spreading the idea that humans have no impact on climate change has a domino effect. A survey by *The Guardian* in 2013 found that ninety-seven percent of climate science papers agree global warming is man-made.[29] Nevertheless, American public opinion on this is split, with a 2012 Gallup Poll showing that only fifty-three percent of Americans believe it primarily results from human activities.[30] This confusion combined with the demand for cheap energy makes it difficult for politicians to curtail energy use among Americans. Without the support of the United States, it has been impossible to take meaningful steps to reduce world carbon dioxide emissions.

When we do think about environmental problems, we focus on a few of them, forgetting the rest and simply ignoring interactions between them. Currently, while some thought is given to global warming and a few other issues such as extreme weather events, a plethora of other planetary problems are overlooked. Together these less prominent but serious problems will place a heavy burden on the future.

We also ignore history, although there is a lot we could learn from it. It presents us with examples of what can happen when people ignore serious threats to their future. Past societies such as those of the Harappan Indus Valley, Easter Island, and the Mayans mismanaged their land as their populations grew. When their lands simply could no longer sustain them, their civilizations collapsed. The ruins of civilizations like these fascinate us, but we have not profited from from their experiences.

The history of environmental ignorance. Information about environmental problems and climate change has been out there for a long time. In 1896 Swedish chemist Svante Arrhenius, and in 1899 American geologist T. C. Chamberlain, unbeknownst to one another, suggested that the burning of fossil fuels might increase global temperatures by increasing the level of carbon dioxide in the atmosphere. In 1957, a study conducted

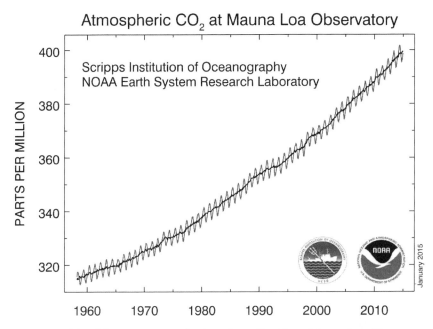

Figure 18. Monthly mean atmospheric carbon dioxide at Mauna Loa Observatory, Hawaii.

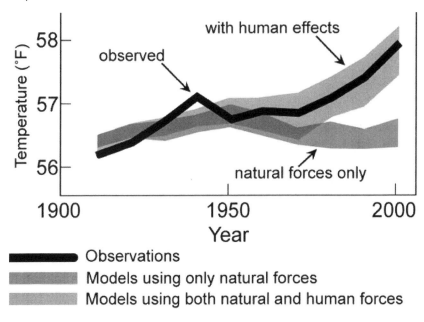

Figure 19. Natural and human influences on global temperature.[23] National Oceanic and Atmospheric Administration, Earth System Research Laboratory.

Figure 20. The once forested Easter Island today. Photo by Bjørn Christian Tørrissen/Wikimedia Commons

by the Scripps Institute of Oceanography Research in California indicated that roughly half of the carbon dioxide released into the atmosphere stayed there. Humanity, the study noted, was "engaged in a great geophysical experiment." In 1965 a White House report to President Johnson devoted 23 of its 291 pages to this topic.[31] It warned that by the year 2000 atmospheric carbon dioxide "may be sufficient to produce measurable and perhaps marked changes in climate, and will almost certainly cause significant changes in temperature and other properties of the stratosphere." We have not yet taken these warnings seriously.

After all these years with snowballing evidence, our political leaders refuse to face this issue; and nations, rather than working together for our common good, refuse to cooperate in a meaningful way to deal with this critical problem.

In 1948 ecologist Fairfield Osborn in his popular book, *Our Plundered Planet,* warned "...that if we continue to disregard nature and its principles the days of our civilization are numbered." He described the problems of overcrowding, soil depletion, and forest destruction. In that same year ornithologist William Voght's book *Road to Survival* appeared, which described similar problems. The well-known writer and editor Clifton Fadiman noted, "*Road to Survival* should—and I think it will—arouse all Americans to a consciousness of how we are ruining the very soil beneath our feet and thereby committing suicide, not too slowly either. Let us hope it will energize a rescue squad, 140,000,000 strong."[32] Despite *Road to Survival* being a Book-of-the-Month-Club selection, Fadiman's hope turned out to be wishful thinking. And now there are 314 million of us.

Although we are doing some things to alleviate these threats, our response to all the evidence of what is happening around us today can best be described as pathetic. The media, the source of much information that reaches the public, haven't helped. Over the years they just haven't seen the environment as important, but as just another issue. Meager coverage does not arouse public concern.

Complexity

The cosmos is extremely complex, ranging from the smallest units of energy to the universe, or universes. Until the introduction of agriculture and later the Industrial Revolution, humans fit into an ecological niche on planet Earth with a hospitable environment provided by Gaia. We did not have to concern ourselves with things beyond our immediate needs. That was all taken care of, and we were not in a position to harm the environment that provided for us. Now with the overwhelming impact humanity has on the planet we have changed all of that. For us to survive, we have to face up to something we never had to before, complexity in its broadest sense. The world we live in, already too intricate for our minds to deal with, is rapidly growing more complex, at a geometric rate. Our tendency to focus on one problem at a time without seeing the whole and the broad range of consequences of what we are doing can lead to other problems.

The everyday world we now live in requires dealing with a vast array of interrelated factors including human behavior that have to be dealt with in a positive way. This can, for example, involve enacting burdensome regulations and controls focused on individual problems that can among other things kill creativity and much of the satisfaction we find in our work. In architecture, my original occupation, for example, the complex sets of necessary regulations that govern building construction consume huge amounts of designers' time and often leave little room for innovation. We must find ways to manage to live safely in a complicated world without destroying new ideas and the joys of working and living.

To deal with our modern world we have developed increasingly intricate systems such as power grids, the Internet, various types of data storage, new ways of doing financial transactions, etc. As these systems become more complicated and integrated into our daily lives, governments, and business, they need large numbers of highly trained specialists to deal with them. As complexity increases, it will probably be harder to find and train enough capable people to develop and maintain these systems effectively. They also become more vulnerable to breakdowns and attacks by hostile governments and sociopaths.

Overload

We can only deal with a limited number of things at once, and only a few of them effectively. If, as good citizens, we seriously concern ourselves not just with our children's education and other needs, but starving Africans, human rights in Central America, the economy, the preservation of historic buildings, cruelty to animals, the welfare system, and antibiotic-resistant bacteria, we saddle ourselves with more than we can possibly deal with and risk becoming neurotic and ineffective. However, without public understanding and concern, critical issues do not receive support. Our inability to focus on and care about a broad range of issues at one time is a big problem today, especially when they keep increasing in number and gravity, and public support for every one of them is essential.

Increasingly more problems, more technology, and more opportunities are piling up on us. But this is not all there is to it. We cannot ignore how things interact and affect each other, and then we must utilize what we learn in our current economic and political climate, which is often very difficult. This presents the public with more things to know and think about; teachers with more to teach; journalists with more to report on, much of which they don't understand; and governments with more things to manage than politics will allow them to deal with in a reasonable way.

If we were constantly aware of everything that needs to be dealt with, we would be so overloaded with information and stimuli that we simply could not function. When the amount of relevant information is too large and the relationships too complex, our brain selects, eliminates, and simplifies to a level that we can handle. But even with our mind's ability to filter input, we are still burdened with huge amounts of data, much of it superfluous, and much of it hard to correlate and utilize.

When journalists do not consistently remind us of situations such as the loss of biodiversity, increasing discipline problems in school, and poorly stored nuclear wastes, they fade from the public mind and politicians' agendas. Concerned individuals and advocacy organizations tend to direct their attention to no more than several issues, such as air pollution or inner city schools, leaving other issues and most importantly, broad overviews, unaddressed. There is never enough time or money to deal with all that we want to, or must, so wherever we can, we ignore or put off for tomorrow.

Ethics and values

In his book *The Story of the Human Body*, human evolutionary biologist Daniel E. Lieberman wrote about our species, "And we not only evolved to cooperate, innovate, communicate, and nurture, but also to cheat, steal, lie, and murder. The bottom line is that many human adaptations did not necessarily evolve to promote physical or mental well-being."[33]

Of the many obstacles to responsible behavior we face, some of the most difficult to overcome are probably those involving ethics. Even when we learn how to solve serious problems, some people simply may choose not to comply. They may not care about other people, such as those who are powerless as well as those of future generations, who have no way to get back at us for injury we may inflict on them. Unfortunately these self-centered individuals, not held back by concerns beyond their own interests, can focus their efforts and energy on achieving their own ends while altruistic individuals with broader concerns spread their time and energy over larger areas.

A vast gulf separates the world of the fortunate from those living in great need and desperation, and much of humanity accepts this and lets it continue.

There is evidence of intended malevolence all around us. Food and medicine containers are sealed to prevent antisocial individuals from introducing poisons such as was done to capsules of Extra-Strength Tylenol in Chicago in 1982. Items in stores are securely enclosed in packages that will set off an alarm if one takes them from the store without paying. We cannot fly or enter a federal building without passing through security checks. Important politicians and many entertainers are protected by guards. Security cameras are everywhere. We need virus and malware programs to protect our computers, and we occasionally find pages ripped out of library and phone books. When catastrophes like floods strike, looters appear to take what they can from those already victimized by the disaster. During wars, when people should be cooperating together, profiteers and black marketers make hay. Unethical activities cost society dearly, not just the direct costs, but also in time and money spent to combat them.

From my own observations few of us are completely honest and can always be trusted. On the other hand, a number of us are outright crooks, and about four percent are sociopaths.[34] Most of us fall somewhere in between—in the middle or towards one end or the other. In his book, *The Selfish Gene,* Richard Dawkins demonstrates how evolution maintains a balance between selfishness and altruism in the human population. [35] Those who lie and cheat have decided advantages, although people look for individuals they can trust, and this benefits the honest. Unfortunately evildoers, by using tactics well-intended people abhor, can often overwhelm the efforts of those who promote peace, stability, and benevolence.

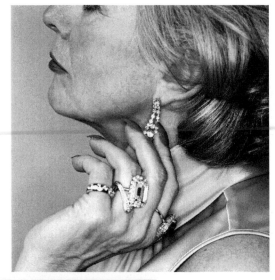

Right: Figure 21. Enjoying some of the "better" things of life. Photo by Kelvin Murray/Getty Images

Below: Figure 22. Malnourished children, weakened by hunger. Photo by Cate Turton/ Department for International Development

Religion and other beliefs

Many people see religions as the backbone of ethical behavior. That may be true; however there are highly ethical atheists and religious beliefs can lead to persecution, intolerance, war, and terrorism. Today some extreme fundamentalist Muslims feel their religion compels them to kill infidels who stand in the way of spreading Islam or who merely violate its values; they will be rewarded in heaven for doing so. And not long ago Protestant and Catholic zealots were killing each other in Ireland, and hundreds of years before that in various parts of Europe. Many of the worst wars humanity has had, and tortures inflicted, were done in the name of God. Blaise Pascal wrote, "Men never do evil so completely and cheerfully as when they do it from religious conviction."

Genesis 2:28 has had a powerful influence on the ethics of many Christians, "...Be fruitful, and multiply, and replenish the earth, and subdue it: and have dominion over the fish of the sea, and over the fowl of the air, and over every living thing that moves upon the earth." In contrast, Chief Seattle of the Suquamish Tribe had a different point of view. He is reported to have said, "This we know—the earth does not belong to man; man belongs to the earth."[36] Jains, members of an Indian religious sect, go even further. Besides refusing to eat animal products, some wear facemasks to avoid breathing in and killing insects, and try not to step in puddles where other creatures might get squashed. Unfortunately, such views are overwhelmed by the baser drives and beliefs of most other people. While we profess respect for the teachings of great religious and ethical leaders, our pursuit of material goods, fostered by advertising, largely obliterates their messages.

Ethical considerations diminish with distance and differences in religion, ethnocentricity, and culture. Except for our own children and grandchildren, we give little thought or consideration to those who will follow us.

Governmental and national ethics

Besides their personal integrity, and for some politicians how they may look in history books, there are few incentives for politicians or corporate executives to care about what happens beyond the next five to ten years. It is hard to expect them to do more in this highly competitive world where people expect results now and reward them for that. Most of the unstated real goals of a nation are neither those of its most noble citizens nor even the higher aspirations of the common person. They are more likely to be those of the politically and economically powerful and the average or baser wants of the public. Whatever they are, they become honorable when they favor the homeland. We like this, for we can let loose our primitive impulses, get what we *think* we want, and be proud of our country.

When our government says that it is acting "in the national interest," it is often giving an ethical ring to what is simply selfishness. Supporting such action becomes patriotism. Questioning such activity is a nonquestion and conducting government on an ethical basis can be suicide for a politician. Should a government conduct its international relations on a strictly ethical basis, there would be a huge public outcry.

We allow and even expect governments to do things we do not permit ourselves to do. War, which is murder unless it is in self-defense, becomes acceptable if it is in "the national interest." Aggression can always be presented as furthering this end. For most people hypocrisy, lying, deceit, and clandestine operations carried out against other nations are seen as normal, necessary activities of governments and of the people who run them. Special interests are always working on leaders to set things up to favor themselves. This introduces unethical behavior into governments.

As centers of power and wealth, governments are honey pots for the greedy. In attempts to counteract corruption and cheating, with limited success, governments have instituted rules, reviews, investigations, rigid procedures, and lengthy forms to fill out. These consume a significant portion of a government's resources and talent, making it hard for it to perform its duties effectively and efficiently.

Hunger for power and resources coupled with humankind's attraction to competition and conflict have fostered wars throughout history. The inevitable clash between growing populations in a world of diminishing natural resources and water and food shortages will surely be a leading cause for wars in the future.

Evolution enables both ethical and unethical behaviors to be passed on. Human society and our planet could tolerate this when weapons were less dangerous and humanity could not harm the entire planet. Today we have weapons that can wipe out most life on Earth, and we are damaging the planet in a way that if continued will make it unlivable. We are, thoughtlessly and irresponsibly, holding the future of our species and of our planet in our hands. General Omar Bradley put it this way, "The world has achieved brilliance without conscience. Ours is a world of nuclear giants and ethical infants. We know more about war than we know about peace, more about killing than we know about living. We have grasped the mystery of the atom and rejected the Sermon on the Mount."

Unintended side effects of good intentions

Ethical behavior, a good thing in itself, can cause more harm than good when it is undertaken without considering the broad picture. Well-intended efforts to help people that fail to address causes of problems can be damaging, for example. We want to provide food and medicine to people who are starving. But without providing them with means for controlling their numbers, this can result in far greater misery as time passes and there are larger numbers of people who will not have enough to eat. In this case, our efforts to do good work against nature's laws where individual welfare is subordinated to that of the species and the planet's ecosystems. When these are altered, they will come back to haunt us. This is a dilemma we avoid talking or thinking about.

We show little feeling or responsibility toward those we are bringing into this world we are so drastically changing. We feel an obligation to allow people to have as many children as they can produce, and we will meagerly support them if their parents can't or won't. On the other hand we feel no obligation to assure that the not yet conceived or born will be brought up by good, healthy, drug-free, loving parents on an earth that is not over-populated. We don't think about what the future holds for abused, unloved, uncared-for children as they grow up and produce more children of their own. The parents are with us now; their future children are not. It would be interesting to know how many unwanted children are born into this world because their parents had no access to means of birth control or abortion, and how this affects the growth rate of the world's population.

And here is something else that deserves attention. Experience has shown us that characteristics of species of plants or animals can be changed within a few generations by selective breeding. Applying this to humanity is taboo and raises appalling thoughts, considering how the Nazis experimented with this. Nevertheless, for the sake of future generations, we should give some thought to which segments of our population are producing the largest number of offspring and which the least.

Ethics in business

My father found great pleasure first in selling, and later in tanning leather. He enjoyed his work, was not greedy, and liked the people he did business with. Enjoyment of the work drives much that is done in business, but money is another motivation, and for some people, the only one. The opportunity to reap huge profits and beat the other guy attracts many unethical people into business.

Being ruthless, willing to backstab, brown nose, cheat, bribe, etc., helps some individuals climb ladders. Even when operating within ethical standards, the competitive nature of commerce and the risk of failure help drive businesspeople to push to the limits on restrictions and ethical behavior. As the influence of business is far-reaching, this can spread poison into society.

As an architect I had to be constantly vigilant of contractors who were trying to cut corners. The temptation to do so is strong as every dollar saved is pure profit. In bidding for jobs, sometimes contractors have to bid against others whom they know will try to underbid them by cutting corners during construction. The problem of the honest having to compete against cost-cutting chiselers is a problem that persists in many areas of business. As many greedy individuals are attracted to business, cheating appears in many places and at the highest levels.

Every year, around the world, about three million people die of tobacco-related diseases. It would be interesting to read in the annual report of a tobacco company: "Last year was a good year; we made roughly $22,000 for every U.S. death that could statistically be attributed to our cigarettes. Fortunately we were not held responsible for the medical costs of these deaths. They were paid by the people themselves or our government." This may sound wild, but check it out; find the numbers and you can calculate it.

If you or I were to go out on the street and shoot someone, we would be sentenced to life in prison or even be executed. When the officers of a corporation, in order to make a profit, foster activities that lead to the painful deaths of many thousands of people, or more, they may be rewarded by handsome salaries, respect, and status. It seems to me this is exactly the case, for example, with the managers of large American tobacco companies, their lobbyists, and their supporters in Congress. When the executives of the major tobacco companies in the United States testified before Congress that tobacco was neither habit-forming nor did it cause cancer, they were not punished for lying even though they had all seen reports showing this to be the case.

Today, fossil fuel companies are behaving the same way by funding efforts to confuse the public by claiming that human activity has no effect on global warming. This effort is playing a significant role in delaying

Figure 23. On April 14, 1994, seven executives from Big Tobacco defended their deadly products before a congressional subcommittee, raising their right hands and swearing that nicotine was not addictive. Their own company documents showed otherwise. Quoting William Campbell, president and CEO of Philip Morris USA, "I believe nicotine is not addictive." The same statement was subsequently made by other executives before television cameras. None were ever charged with perjury. Photo by John Duricka/AP

steps to control climate change, which will cause terrible misery for billions of people in the future while it reaps huge profits for their industry over the next few years. Is money all that matters to these people? Don't they even care about their own grandchildren? Cigarette company executives can tell their children not to smoke. The grandchildren of fossil fuel executives cannot escape the planet; perhaps the executives feel their descendants' money will help them avoid what others will suffer.

Large numbers of people admire the rich and powerful, no matter how they reached their goal. CEOs are compensated many multiples of what significant contributors to society earn—teachers, scientists, artists, and medical workers, for example. What has happened to the teachings of Jesus and Gandhi, and our values?

Corruption in business

When many businesspersons run into things they don't like, such as restrictions and taxes, if they have enough money, they find politicians eager to fill their campaign coffers who will get laws changed or provide new ones they like. When this activity is widespread as it is in the U.S. today, I find it hard to believe that we still have a democracy; it is an oligarchy! From what I see, corruption is the norm, and it takes unrelenting vigilance and effort to minimize it.

Major General Smedley Darlington Butler was at the time of his death the most decorated Marine in U.S. history. In 1935 he wrote *War Is a Racket*, an exposé of the profit motive behind warfare. His views were summarized in the socialist magazine *Common Sense*:[14]

"I spent 33 years and four months in active military service and during that period I spent most of my time as a high-class muscle man for Big Business, for Wall Street and the bankers.

"In short, I was a racketeer, a gangster for capitalism. I helped make Mexico and especially Tampico safe for American oil interests in 1914. I helped make Haiti and Cuba a decent place for the National City Bank boys to collect revenues in. I helped in the raping of half a dozen Central American republics for the benefit of Wall Street. I helped purify Nicaragua for the International Banking House of Brown Brothers in 1902-1912. I brought light to the Dominican Republic for the American sugar interests in 1916. I helped make Honduras right for the American fruit companies in 1903. In China in 1927 I helped see to it that Standard Oil went on its way unmolested. Looking back on it, I might have given Al Capone a few hints. The best he could do was to operate his racket in three districts. I operated on three continents." A similar story regarding his work is told by economist John Perkins in *Confessions of an Economic Hitman*, published by Plume in 2005. By cooking the books he helped U.S. intelligence agencies and multinationals cajole and blackmail foreign leaders into awarding lucrative contracts to American businesses and serving U.S. foreign policy.

OUR ORGANIZATIONS

As human social evolution advanced, societies needed more expertise than any single person could possess. Evolution found the solution in specialization. Individuals developed skills in specific directions and learned to rely on other people for skills they themselves did not possess. This made it possible for families and societies to have more capabilities than any single individual could have. In families, different tasks were performed by men, women, the young, and the elderly. In groups, some people became chiefs, priests, healers, warriors, hunters, or gatherers. Specialization is not unique to humans; it is very apparent in ant and termite colonies and between the sexes in many species.

Carl Gustav Jung, Katharine Cook Myers, Walter Lowen,[37] and most recently my late friend Alan Kahn[38] recognized and wrote about our tendency to rely on a a variety of different approaches for dealing with the world. Systems scientist Walter Lowen defined sixteen personality types arranged into pairs with opposing characteristics, combined in different ways. Strengths in one direction generally leave us weaker in the opposite. Some of us are good at working with people (social worker or salesperson), others with things (engineer or carpenter). Others like to think abstractly (mathematician or political scientist) or concretely (businessperson or baker). Some people feel comfortable dealing with a number of things at once (receptionist or manager), others like to to concentrate on a single task until it is finished and then move on to another (scientist or writer).

Opportunities are missed and problems arise when people occupy positions for which they are they are ill suited. This can go beyond poor performance to causing serious harm when positions affecting policy and important operations of government are filled with individuals who don't understand how things really work. In these difficult and dangerous times society needs the most intelligent, informed, altruistic, and competent leadership available. This is hardly the case.

LEADERSHIP AND FOLLOWERSHIP

Doers versus thinkers

Some people are curious and devote much time to learning about the world around them and on thinking about how conditions might be improved. We can call these people "thinkers." They recognize that complicated problems rarely have simple cures. While these people often lack leadership ability or talent for getting things done, they generally have the best understanding of problems and the clearest ideas on how they might be resolved. Some people enjoy action and are good at it and focus on getting things done. We can call these people "doers." Their consuming interests in these areas, and the energy they expend on them, generally preclude them from being serious thinkers. Their curiosity is focused more on how to accomplish things and how to achieve their ends than on what should best be done.

Some doers concentrate on pursuing wealth, power, or fame. They are often successful at gaining it, particularly when not hampered by conscience. As a result, the world is largely run by them. Because they spend their time and energy on getting things done, their knowledge in many areas is limited. They may have little understanding of the implications of what they are dealing with and fail to recognize their own shortcomings. Often they need to make quick decisions, like simplistic answers to complex questions, and give little thought to the distant future.

Herbert A. Simon, Nobel Prize winner in economics, wrote of this type in his book *Administrative Behavior*. "Administrative man recognizes that the world he perceives is a drastically simplified model of the buzzing, blooming confusion that constitutes the real world. He is content with this gross simplification because he believes that the real world is mostly empty—that most of the facts of the real world have no great relevance to any particular situation he is facing and that most significant chains of causes and consequences are short and simple. Hence he is content to leave out of account those aspects of reality—and that means most aspects—that appear irrelevant at a given time. He makes his choices using a simple picture of the situation that takes into account just a few of the factors that he regards as most relevant and crucial."[39]

Businesspeople and politicians generally think like this. They are the people who run things and get things done—or prevent them from getting done. Because they are successful and powerful, and because they think that what they themselves are good at is what is important, many of them view scientists and other "thinkers" as ineffectual, irrelevant, irritating, and not worth listening to. They look for answers they like, not wishing to be distracted by the wide range of inputs that exist in reality, such as the effect of dropping water tables on economic growth, for example. When they look for advice, they generally turn to people who share their opinions and tell them what they want to hear, or who can tell them how to maintain or increase their power or wealth.

Governors on motors and thermostats on furnaces are important parts of negative feedback loops that prevent motors from speeding out of control and houses from overheating. In the same way, information about our effect on the environment should be sent back to those who have the largest roles in managing human society. However, the arrogance of doers regularly prevents this from working. They ignore critical information provided by evidence and thinkers. Consequently, we are a species running out of control.

Who gains positions of leadership

In democracies we get to choose political candidates from a list of mostly ambitious individuals who have an appetite for power or a desire to be important, and who have spent much of their time building political support. The selection process in totalitarian countries and those in a state of chaos is far worse.

People who desire and attain power are likely to spend much, if not most, of their time gaining and then bolstering their power base and honing their political skills. This leaves them with too little time to understand the world and its nonpolitical problems. Politics draws competitive people who often like confrontation. It tends to eliminate the cooperative individuals we desperately need today. They don't want to participate in the selection process—or cannot.

Superior individuals who have the qualities we need in our current complex world are not likely to run for office or become autocrats. They do not want to subject themselves to the hassles necessary to succeed in politics, are not prone to win the support of special-interest groups, nor are they likely to have wide public appeal. We thus have a mechanism that fills positions of power with people who can effectively deal with each other in their dog-eat-dog world, but are poorly equipped to understand, and have little interest in, the complexity of many matters affecting our future. These are the people who have the most influence on the relationships between nations and cultures, and our relationship to our planet as well.

The resulting dilemma

Governments and many businesses are run by highly competitive individuals. Winning takes precedence over cooperation. This helps to explain why well thought out plans requiring international cooperation presented by citizens' groups, scientists, and the like are rejected by those holding political power. Climate change is an example. In the Asahi Glass Foundation of Tokyo, Japan's *Questionnaire on Environmental Problems and the Survival of Humankind* [40] participants indicated that there was a huge gap between government and business, and scientists and individuals concerned about the environment.

The people we must depend on to make important, complex decisions regarding our future are some of the least able or willing to understand the threats to it, or to register concern for it. In politics a limited viewpoint is often essential. To succeed, one must quickly recognize opportunities for advantage and react to them. Few people, including politicians, look beyond the parts to see the big picture. As it is rare for outstanding human beings to reach points of power, we are often dependent on mediocre, myopic minds to make important decisions affecting the future of humanity and of our planet. The late economist Kenneth Boulding, who was interested in the selection process, had this to say. "There is indeed a principle which I have called the 'dismal theorem of political science'—that most of the skills which lead to the rise to power unfit people to exercise it."[41] Adlai Stevenson, an unsuccessful candidate for president who had strong support among the well educated, when interviewed by Bill Moyers commented, "By the time a man is elected president he is no longer worthy of the office."

We continually show that we do not want superior individuals to lead us. Psychologist C. A. Gibb puts it succinctly, "The evidence suggests that every increment of intelligence means wiser government, but that the crowd prefers to be ill-governed by people it can understand."[42]

The commonplace citizen

The Spanish philosopher Ortega y Gasset described the average person this way. "The mass is...those who demand nothing special of themselves, but for whom to live is to be every moment what they are, without imposing on themselves any effort towards perfection; mere buoys that float on the waves."[43] He portrayed the problem of the modern world as this: "The characteristic of the hour is the commonplace mind, knowing itself to be commonplace, has the assurance to proclaim the rights of the commonplace and to impose them where ever it will.... The mass crushes beneath it everything that is different, everything that is excellent, individual, qualified and select. Anybody who is not like everybody, who does not think like everybody, runs the risk of being eliminated."[44] The situation has not gotten any better since he wrote this.

While the "masses" ask little of themselves, they have simple but unrealizable expectations of their leaders. Prominent among their demands

Figure 24. Painting by William Hogarth ca. 1755, "An Election Entertainment." Wikimedia Commons

are perpetual prosperity, security, comfort, and entertainment. Can one blame them? They tend to give their allegiance to politicians who flatter their ignorance and apathy and promise to meet their unreasonable demands. As well intended as most people may be, their drives and goals are dangerous in this world today.

"Leadership" by inaction

We often prefer inaction on the part of our leaders. Even when we recognize a serious problem such as the greenhouse effect, considering how the measures to deal with it might affect us, we may want them to ignore it. We like to have our desires satisfied now, and expecting tomorrow to take care of itself, we refuse to accept accountability for our own future. We are opting for short-term gratification and staking our future on the hope that everything will "work out" if the economy grows. Successful leaders know this (think this way themselves) and gain our favor by supporting our irresponsibility.

We all follow each other

Except at our own peril, we must all, leaders and led, journalists and businesspeople, satisfy the desires of those upon whom we depend, no matter how uninformed they are or how perverse their desires may be. The British diplomat Benjamin Disraeli put it this way, "I must follow the people. Am I not their leader?" Politicians do and say what is needed to get our votes. We do not like them for that, but we vote for them because they do.

In democracies political leaders are under enormous pressure to meet public demands. They must promise prosperity and avoid dealing with unpleasant subjects like fiscal responsibility, raising taxes, conserving resources, and a more equitable sharing of the world's wealth. We not only like politicians who promise good things—we want to believe them. Many people tend to think that politicians understand what they talk about and do. What they actually do know is largely what is needed to win the next election, and what they do is largely what ingratiates them with their financial backers, and to a lesser degree us.

In a democracy, citizens are supposedly the source of power, however they are very successfully manipulated by specialists employed by businesspeople and politicians. But the politicians and businesspeople are following the people, and journalists complete the circle. With few exceptions, everyone is watchfully following someone else, like the tigers in *Little Black Sambo*.

THE WORKINGS OF GOVERNMENT

"If men were angels, no government would be necessary. If angels were to govern men, neither external nor internal controls on government would be necessary. In framing a government which is to be administered by men over men, the great difficulty lies in this: you must first enable the government to control the governed; and in the next place oblige it to control itself." James Madison, *The Federalist Papers*. It is clear that one of the main goals of governments today is to maintain the positions of the people who run them.

The myth of an informed citizenry

For a democracy to work as it should, there must be an informed citizenry that acts responsibly and ethically to further not just its own welfare, but the overall good. As I have previously pointed out, most people's knowledge and interests have little to do with survival. Few people read, watch, or listen to things that challenge their beliefs or lifestyle. Many people are not interested in, nor do they even have a rudimentary understanding of complex subjects. Most citizens and their political leaders embrace ideas such as "our nation above all," or "cutting taxes creates jobs." As Isaac Asimov noted, "There is a cult of ignorance in the United States, and there always has been. The strain of anti-intellectualism has been a constant thread winding its way through our political and cultural life, nurtured by the false notion that democracy means that 'my ignorance is just as good as your knowledge.' "[45]

The craving for personal gain and security, on the part of politicians as well as many individuals, exceeds their commitment to the democratic process. Politicians and special interests can often achieve their ends by deceiving the public about what is right and what benefits it. People are thus cheated out of exactly what a democracy is intended to do for them.

In democracies, politicians cannot appeal to reason and good sense from a largely ignorant, malleable, apathetic electorate misled by special interests, and motivated by primitive drives, personal and group agendas. and religious beliefs that ignore reality. A misinformed public and selfish special interests exert enormous pressure on governments to meet their demands on issues they may not fully understand, but see as important to themselves. There are always reasons, war and recession for example, to divert attention from serious problems such as environmental degradation. This leaves little time without such happenings for governments to focus on such serious problems. In dictatorships autocrats are not interested in dealing with the reality of the physical world; they focus on maintaining their hold on power.

Governance by the lowest common denominator

In a democracy the commonplace majority and special interests set the agenda that politicians must address. Even when a politician knows that humanity is contributing to climate change, in order to secure campaign funding and be reelected she feels compelled to limit discussion to a few topics, generally aspects of material well-being, fear, security, and subjects of concern to special-interest groups.

When in office the mechanics of democratic governments also limit what politicians can do. They can, within departments, fund studies, demand reports, and hold conferences on serious matters. But ultimately, they are restricted by what political procedures and their citizens allow. Senator Al Gore observed, "Ironically, at this stage, the maximum that is politically feasible still falls short of the minimum that is truly effective."[46]

Because of how our minds and democratic government now work, Congress and the president must confine their attention to a few major problems at one time—such as those of the budget or crime. Action on complex, controversial issues that require time-consuming public and legislative debate and carry political risks is easily put off.

Objective problem-solving in government is next to impossible. Politics makes it difficult to present data accurately. Who says something, how well it is said, how closely it conforms to truisms and personal agendas, and how often it is repeated have considerably more impact on us than reason and the validity of the data itself. To make topics suitable for public discussion and within the interests of politicians, often some of the most critical issues are simply ignored. Repetition of positions and slogans overshadows reason.

As a result of all of the above, many important issues are ignored, misunderstood, or mismanaged. Once we could get by in this way; however today, because of the number and magnitude of the problems we face, we cannot. When humans lived in a simpler world they could bungle along like this. Faced with threats like climate change, overpopulation, water shortages, and weapons of mass destruction that few people comprehend the seriousness of, this is no longer the case.

Serious consequences

An uninformed, irresponsible public places demands on governments that can only be met by ignoring the future, the environment, and international cooperation. Thus the "circle of followership" leaves us in a dangerous position today. We are like a little dog that chases its tail while a big dog (serious environmental threats) is pursuing it. Most politicians choose to react to issues set before them and solve current crises rather than look down the road, see what's coming, and deal with it in a constructive, cooperating way. This behavior leaves us adrift in a world of dangerous threats with no real leadership. As an architect who found great satisfaction in facing and solving problems, I find it hard to see a responsible explanation for this.

What governments used to do no longer works

What governments could once do easily and well no longer works. Until recently democratic and autocratic governments could get by doing what they do, often with great injustice and human misery, but without setting off a global nuclear war or seriously damaging our planet as a healthy place for life. This has changed. The human world has become huge and complex with powerful weapons and tools at its disposal; simple solutions to major threats no longer work. In a democracy scientifically ignorant, arrogant, irrational leadership can lead to drastic planetary harm.

Governments composed of officials fixed on their own well-being, and depending on funding from special-interest groups and a public demanding immediate rewards for their support are unlikely to function in a wise, foresighted way. The desire to hold political office becomes the overwhelming priority for some officials and regularly outweighs the need to deal with critical problems, the welfare of their constituents, and concern for the future. After the 2010 elections when many "Tea Party" candidates won seats in Congress, Republicans who had recognized that climate change was partly caused by human activity, concerned about future votes, quickly changed their "beliefs." This has reset the current Republican Party's agenda on climate change, and is blocking any significant U.S. agreement to a worldwide protocol to contain global warming.

When people don't bother to inform themselves on all sides of an issue, but demand quick, easy fixes and perpetual prosperity, they are asking politicians to deceive them. Consequently, politicians tell us what we want to hear and flatter our shortcomings. The term "the silent majority" glorifies apathy and ignorance.

Nations refuse to cooperate

Within their borders, as noted earlier, nations have laws and regulations, backed up by police, to maintain order. They have armies to protect themselves from other nations and peoples. However they refuse to cooperate to maintain world peace and work together to prevent the kinds of wars we have had in recent history.

As long as the world is divided into sovereign nations, we will have what the noted political scientist John Herz called the "security dilemma." Quoting him, "The 'security dilemma' besets, above all, those units which, in their respective historical setting, are the highest ones, that is, not subordinate to any higher authority. Since, for their protection and even their survival, they cannot rely on any higher authority, they are necessarily thrown back on their own devices; and since they cannot be sure of the intentions of competing units, they must be prepared for 'the worst.' Hence they must have means of defense. But preparing for defense may arouse the suspicions of others, who in turn will engage in such preparation. A vicious cycle will arise—of suspicion and counter-suspicion, competition for power, armament races, ultimately war."[47] We seem to be unable to comprehend the reality of this, or to sensibly weigh the risks we take by tenaciously holding on to our cherished sovereignties.

When dealing with other nations politicians must make it clear that their own country comes first. Cooperation is fine, but not at the expense of one's own country. In an effort to extend order worldwide, the United Nations was established in 1945, a grand attempt to make some sense out of the international free-for-all. Good as this may be, in the United States, and elsewhere, politicians cannot be seen as forgoing any of their sovereignty for the overall good.

The unwillingness of nations to cooperate on controlling fish catches has left some of the most popular varieties of fish nearly depleted in the world's oceans. At the Kyoto and Copenhagen Climate Change Conferences participating countries made sure not to give away things that were dear to them, like in the United States, our lifestyle, and in China, their potential to become like the United States. We have learned much more about climate change since 1997, and it is looking worse than we previously had thought; nevertheless we are no closer to coming to a substantial, meaningful agreement than we were then.

Institutionalized violence

While humans readily take to violence on an individual level, we also do it collectively, such as the actions of some ethnic or religious groups, and the organized violence done by governments such as war or ethnic cleansing. Wars can result from disputes over land or resources, ethnic conflicts, past disputes, ambitious, tyrannical leaders, and a host of other things that can all too easily lead to violent confrontation. Dissimilar religious, political, and economic groups or beliefs erect barriers and misunderstandings between people, increasing the possibility of violence on a small or grand scale. A world divided into camps of zealots ready to convert or conquer is a dangerous one.

Hostility, even without confrontation, can produce damage that can continue over long periods of time. During the Cold War, the USSR and the United States ignored many pressing problems while they diverted huge amounts of money and talent to producing weapons and arming seemingly peaceful nations. They left a legacy of toxic chemical and nuclear waste, pollution, and antiquated factories that will be a burden for nations on into the future. Buried land mines and unexploded bombs left by armies and terrorists will threaten farmers and others for many decades to come.

When peoples' lives are difficult, they want simple answers. They become willing to listen to demagogues, eager to blame scapegoats, and ready to use force. "Bad times," instability, fear, hate, chauvinism, and peer pressure work together to enable a small number of individuals to seize political power and create dangerous hostilities. Many nations and cultures, perhaps most, have idealized and glorified war and at times aggression. There are monuments, songs, paintings, stories, movies, and operas that celebrate it.

We are good at waging first-class wars, but are only willing to pay for fourth-class peace. According to www.GlobalSecurity.org, in 2011 the world spent $2,157,172,000,000, which is 3.1 percent of its gross domestic product, for military purposes.

Damage from a distance

In hunting-gathering societies people faced their enemies. In our technological world of international conflicts, the perpetrator is often separated from his victim, who is invisible to him. It is often the least imaginative and empathetic among us who hold power and will affect those they have no connection to nor feeling for. The perpetrator functions like a bureaucrat "just doing his job," as Martin Bormann, the Nazi exterminator of Jews, put it.

In 1941 George Orwell, the British novelist and essayist, wrote in "England Your England," "As I write, highly civilized human beings are flying overhead trying to kill me. They do not feel any enmity to me as an individual, nor I against them. They are only 'doing their duty,' as the saying goes. Most of them, I have no doubt, are law-abiding, kind-hearted men who would never dream of committing murder in private life. On the other hand, if one of them succeeds in blowing me to pieces with a well-placed bomb, he will never sleep the worse for it. He is serving his country, which has the power to absolve him from evil."

Business serves many essential functions in human society. It makes things work, enables us to meet our needs, and fosters efficiency. It also has a profound influence on our culture and mores. Because it is profitable it is respected, admired, and sometimes given credit for possessing capacities beyond what it actually has. It has not been shy about employing public relations firms to boost its image. Its wealthy leaders are listened to by government and citizens alike.

The drive to maximize profits

Maximizing profit can determine what business does. For example, the primary purpose of a business may not be to produce a particular product, but rather to produce top profit. If a bicycle factory can make more money with its assets and know-how selling insurance and moving to a new location, in theory it will do so, as in reality it may choose or be forced to do. Overfishing whales and driving them into extinction makes sense when the high profits gained by overfishing can be reinvested in something else when catches decline. This is neither good for whales nor for whalers, nonetheless it pays off for investors.

Dangers of this. Free enterprise fosters efficiency, which is mostly good. On the other hand, without regulation, it encourages the exploitation of natural and human resources and furthers pollution. An industry can use its profits to influence government to minimize controls. Within an industry where competition is strong, the lowest cost producers prevail. This encourages businesses, no matter how well intended, to spend as little as possible for labor, worker protection, and pollution control to gain an advantage over competitors, or merely to survive.

Because they have accumulated considerable amounts of money, many businesspeople believe their way of thinking is superior to that of people who think in a different way, as I explained earlier. They ignore much that is important for society and tend to value science only when they see money in it, and ignore it when it tells them things they do not like.

What corporations are

When businesses are privately owned their owners are responsible for management. They put their own ethical and personal beliefs about how to run the enterprise into practice. While it is essential to make a profit, considerations such as pride in the product, employee welfare, and community concern can play important parts in what is done. Corporations are owned by investors and are managed by managers who are legally responsible to stockholders to maximize profits without breaking the law. If they do not perform this way, stockholders can take them to court. The pressure to produce profits for shareholders often pushes corporations to break laws where they think they can get away with it. They have a benefit that individual business owners do not have—corporations cannot be jailed. Today the majority of investors keep their money in a corporation for less than a year,[48] and this does not promote concern for anything beyond the next few years.

How they work. Large corporations are not run by their owners. Their owners, the stockholders, focus their interest on profits. They care about how much they themselves will make at an acceptable risk over the period of time they own their stock. For most people, as long as their investment pays well, they do not care what their corporation does or even whether it is disbanded. When they see a better opportunity for themselves, they put their money elsewhere.

Corporations are run by officers and boards of directors interested in their own remuneration. They collect proxies from uninformed owners, get themselves re-elected to office, and award themselves astounding salaries and lucrative perks. The owners do not care as long as profits are good, or share prices rise. The management of large corporations must make it appear that profits will continue to increase over the next few years. They have little incentive to care what happens beyond that when they will be working with a still higher pay package for another corporation, or living in extreme luxury in one of those places the ultra-rich go to spend time with one another. Even though they themselves may wish to address serious long-term goals, it is short-term results that managers are rewarded for.

Corporations harm communities by moving employees in and out and detaching them from their locality and extended families. With minimal regret, sometimes they move management, and occasionally whole businesses, to distant locations. National big box stores cause local businesses to close and replace publicly owned "downtowns" with anonymously owned shopping malls outside of community limits, where the only say local citizens have is through their pocketbook. Hometown talent and local creativity have largely been killed off by big-time whatever brought in from elsewhere. Costs such as these rarely play a part in decisions made by these corporations. Profits are what count; the costs are borne by others. Corporate executives are rewarded for the bottom line, and caring about climate change, pollution, resource depletion, or the well-being of the communities where they do business is a distraction they can be criticized for by stockholders.

Advertising

The market allegedly determines what takes place in the world of commerce. But there is more to it in the real world. Successful businesses are proficient at using advertising and planned obsolescence to increase demand. They are encouraged to do this by the high profits it generates.

Endless commercial messages appealing to our primitive desires cannot but have a negative impact on our values and mores. Advertising impresses on us the idea that happiness comes from owning an expensive new car or drinking a soft drink. In 1941 Erich Fromm wrote of advertising, "As a matter of fact, these methods of dulling the capacity for critical thinking are more dangerous to our democracy than many of the open attacks against it."[49]

By bypassing reason and appealing to our strong primitive urges, advertising induces people to purchase goods and services they do not need or want. Planned obsolescence increases replacement rates either by producing goods with a limited life, or by making them trendy so that one must keep replacing them periodically to stay in fashion. By getting us to consume, consume, and consume, advertising furthers resource depletion, waste, and pollution, increases the rate of global warming, and undermines higher human values. It encourages crime by creating wants beyond what people can afford. We defend advertisers' rights to deface our cities and landscapes with billboards, to fill airwaves with messages, and to clutter our children's minds with what suits their purposes. As our economic system now works, in our democracy we are powerless to control this "free speech," and our economy would crash without it.

THE MEDIA AND EDUCATION

In order for a democracy to work and for us to deal with one another and the world in a rational way, we need accurate information about what is out there and what is happening. Of the many ways we receive our information about the world around us, the media and schools are the most widespread and comprehensive. The news media and the Internet are the fastest way to inform citizens about matters of public concern. Do the media, the "watchdogs of democracy," really provide us with the information we need?

Pressures on the media

To satisfy their audiences and keep their jobs, journalists tend to reflect popular conventional thinking. Few people are interested in serious new ideas or in-depth coverage of issues relating to science, the environment, or education. So what we mostly get is plenty of news about food, celebrities, violence, human-interest stories, and superficial reporting on politics and current events. Newspapers and news programs that have failed to provide what the public wants cater to small or shrinking audiences, or are no longer in business. What is covered, or even mentioned, in newspapers and magazines is also strongly influenced by those who advertise in a publication. Offending or pointing a finger at an advertiser is generally out of the question. Presenting news and information is expensive, and because of the large amounts of money involved, most of the owners of newspapers and television are corporations or wealthy individuals. Producers and anchorpersons on network television news are highly paid. Their high earnings may influence their point of view on what they report. Since the media depend on advertisers for financial support, they cannot help but also be influenced by the business community. Our "watchdogs" are not as free, objective, and critical as we would like them to be.

The nature of journalists

What newspapers and television tell us is also shaped by the personalities of the people who are attracted to media careers. Most journalists think in concrete terms, are fascinated by conflict and politics, are highly oriented to the present, and think in terms of stories, or clearly defined subjects. While some journalists think in broader terms, their work must pass through conventional-thinking editors or producers attuned to their audiences. The need to attract and hold an audience presses journalists to dramatize their subject. This can lead to sensationalizing. Where voice and video are involved, what we receive is also colored by how the voice, appearance, and personality of the presenter affect us.

Unconnected fragments

For the most part news items are presented as pieces with little connection to other things. Consequently the public sees them this way. While there are journalists who specialize, in science for example, the editors who control content are usually people who understand writing, politics, conflict, and public appeal and see them as important, and things like the environment much less so. What we get is filtered though their viewpoints.

Space makes might (and right)

Readers and viewers assess the importance of things largely by the space or time devoted to them. And as most of us—especially advertisers—know, the more often something is repeated, the more we think about it and see it as important. Because the media avoid the issue of overpopulation, many people don't think about it, or see it as a problem. Because few people read or hear that perpetual economic growth in a finite space is impossible, they just don't think about that. As the media provide people with what currently interests them, the public's opinion of what is of great or little consequence is reinforced. Nothing is more important than things that are threatening our planet's future, yet little time, if any at all, is spent describing these problems in outlets such as Fox News—and when they are, it is in a derogatory way.

From 1989 through 1991, television network news spent sixty-seven minutes per month reporting on crime. An ABC poll in June of 1993 showed that five percent of those polled felt that crime was our most important problem. By the end of 1993 crime reporting on the networks had risen to 157 minutes a month. A February 1994 poll showed that crime had become the nation's most serious problem for thirty-one percent of Americans.[50] It went on to become the most important issue during the fall 1994 political campaign. While crime was becoming a major public concern, statistics showed that most forms of it were actually declining.

By January 25, 2008 CBS's Bob Schieffer and Fox News's Chris Wallace had conducted 171 interviews with political candidates. Of the 2975 questions they asked, only six mentioned the words "climate change." When the media, the major informer of adults, does not introduce and show the importance of what's taking place in the world, the public remains largely ignorant and unmoved on matters of critical importance. What we do get is a plethora of information about things and situations we cannot do anything about, while we are told little about seriously threatening environmental problems that need an informed public demanding solutions.

"Balanced" reporting

When covering a subject many reporters take the easy way out by just quoting simplistic statements like, "this bill will never pass as is," or "we have the situation under control," rather than giving us background information and a clear idea of what is really happening. They also regularly give us what they call "balanced" reporting by giving both sides of an argument equal treatment and inadequate reporting on the credentials of the presenters. This sounds objective, but it can be highly misleading. When discussing global warming, for example, some journalists have repeatedly given the comments of a "scientist" sponsored by a think tank with a name like Citizens for a Healthy Environment, largely funded by the fossil fuel industry, equal standing with a scientist highly respected by his peers, who has spent most of his career studying global warming. This kind of balanced reporting has created a huge amount of confusion in the public on subjects like climate change.

Challenging attitudes toward science

The media rarely confront political candidates about their views on scientific issues. I cannot remember a journalist asking a politician in an interview to explain why humans have nothing to do with climate change.

Zealots are deceiving the public today on critical issues by their statements in the media. Some tell us that there is no environmental crisis, that evolution is a hoax, or that the world's population growth will slow down and stop as people in the underdeveloped nations become prosperous. If evidence were presented to the public fairly, it would discredit such claims.

Our current educational system

We rarely make the effort to think rationally. Doing so is hard for us, as noted earlier, and schools don't help us nearly as much as they should. Since clear thinking is essential today, this is astonishing. School teaches us many things about how to get along in our modern consumer society, but little about how our planet works or how we think—which affects how we deal with each other and with our planet. Although basic science is widely taught in the United States, it is often taught poorly by teachers who may have a love and aptitude for words but little for science. Although the consequences of not understanding science can be catastrophic, we show little concern for this deficiency. Large numbers of students apparently come away with the idea that scientific evidence, like the human causes for global warming, can be treated just like another belief. To satisfy my curiosity, I have asked many people to explain the scientific method. Few of them could give me a clear answer.

While education is not a swift fix for our environmental crisis, children do grow up—faster than we expect, it seems. Our past failure to have taught children what they needed to better understand our planet and themselves is one of the major causes for the damage we are currently conflicting on our planet, and our inadequate response to this problem.

Chapter Six

WE CAN CHANGE

It is we humans who have caused most of the problems outlined here, and only we can resolve them. While we are doing many things to reduce environmental threats, it is clear that overall our current efforts are falling short as conditions continue to worsen faster than we are mitigating them.

Warnings from scientists, concerned individuals, and the few journalists who speak out clearly on the subject are ignored by most people and governments. If we just look around, we can observe places in the world where the consequences of overpopulation and environmental degradation have firmly taken hold—Haiti and Bangladesh, for example. However those of us who are not suffering now, particularly those who make important decisions and are basking in luxury, do not feel it.

As the world's population grows, pollution increases, and nations fight over diminishing supplies of food, water, and other natural resources, and mass migrations take place, it will become ever more difficult, if not impossible, to keep our inherent tendencies toward violence and corruption under control. Unfortunately, we give this growing but real possibility very little thought. Our minds are just incapable of imagining half a billion people starving in the future as a drought hits a world already without adequate food supplies. Unless we change direction, we are now headed toward a worldwide collapse with no place left to escape to.

And there are tipping points such as the one suggested by James Hansen. Should we burn all the fossil fuels available to us, it would bring on the Venus syndrome. Other possible tipping points—irreversible positive feedback loops—may emerge from the complex interactions of events increasingly taking place.

When environments change and species fail to adapt, dinosaurs for example, they go extinct. They became extinct because the environment surrounding them changed for reasons beyond their control. Our environment is changing because we are changing it. There is nothing that says that a species cannot bring about its own end. This should give us something to think about. Observable evidence shows that our brains evolved to enable us to function as hunter-gatherers, and the way we use them makes us dangerous misfits in the new environment we have created. We must consciously override habitual ways of thinking that prevent us from working together to safely coexist with one another and our planet today.

What will the Earth be like if we do change?

Many people may harbor the idea that if some of the environmental warnings we hear are correct, when they become apparent to everyone, we can put our American know-how to work and quickly straighten things out as we always have. However, if we did fully apply ourselves now, considering all the damage already done, what is still being done, and the momentum pushing things forward, by the time stability was reached, Earth would be very different than it is today. Current trends show there will be more people living on a more depleted, polluted planet for many decades to come. Today we tend to believe there is a satisfactory solution for everything. This illusion will not hold true in the future as we face increasingly more serious problems and our life on earth becomes more complex and difficult. We will have to accept the best we can get, and the sooner we act the less damage will have been done by the time we achieve sustainability.

Looking at the planet today and what we are doing to it is disturbing; however looking at ourselves is far more disturbing and depressing. To change our course, a significant number of people must revise their mindset. Governments, businesses, and other organizations can then respond, and our hard and soft infrastructures can begin to be restructured for sustainability.

If we are to do better we must look at reality straight on and accept what we are. By doing so we can do the best that is possible, although it may not be all that we currently see as what we want.

Potential for improvement

What I have described in the preceding pages looks very discouraging, and it is. A few years ago I was asked to write a scenario on the demise of the human species. I called my article, "Is It Inevitable That Evolution Self-Destruct?"[51] After giving some thought to the subject, this sounded like a very real possibility. This was a subject I never would have chosen to write about myself. It was extremely depressing, so I was glad when I was later asked to write a piece, later published as, "To Achieve Sustainability."[52] But when I researched how we have been and are now responding to environmental threats, this turned out to be even more depressing.

Nevertheless, we can change direction. Unlike most animals, we have access to a huge inventory of information and can consciously plan our future. And while we cannot have the kind of world we would like fifty years from now, if we recognize where we are headed, and change what is most harmful, there is a good chance that a smaller number of people can live satisfying lives on Earth far into the future. By getting beyond our usual shallow way of thinking, contemplating what really matters in our lives, and taking a broad and realistic view of our situation as it is, we could find much value and satisfaction in life in a less wasteful and sustainable world.

We must make a conscious and successful effort to restore balance to our ecological niche. Without this we cannot achieve sustainability. It will take strong new thinking and commitment added to the efforts that many people are already making today—exerting political pressure, building community gardens, recycling, protecting endangered species, and the like. While these efforts, including those of governments and some businesses, are not keeping up with the damage being done, they are building a base we must expand and branch out from.

WHAT WE NEED TO DO TO CHANGE

Become more than what we are

We cannot be blamed for being what we are—creatures that evolved to function sustainably as hunter-gatherers. In order to safely live in the environment we have created, we must look beyond what we would like to be and come to grips with what we really are. Society needs to publicly recognize that we have not evolved to safely deal with the world as we have changed it, a world well past the point of sustainability. We must make a decision to do better, and then do so.

People need to recognize that someone motivated by primitive drives like pursuing status purely for personal satisfaction or seeking political office just to satisfy their vanity or need for power is acting much like an animal responding to basic instincts. We must come to see such traits in ourselves and others for what they are, and recognize the harm some of them are doing to all of us.

Our conscious mind has to take control over our unconscious, Freud's superego over our id. We must rise above Ortega y Gasset's "mass man" who is perfectly satisfied with being just what he is. Rising above what comes easily to us must be seen by everyone as a necessity, and those who accomplish this should be respected. It won't be easy to get everyone to make the effort to become more than what they are. But considering the consequences of failure, we must try hard.

We need to understand how we interact in groups of all kinds. We should be made aware of our irrational surrender to peer pressure and fads, how we can get caught up in the hysteria of a crowd, and relinquish our personal integrity to a larger entity as some people do when their government fosters atrocities.

Change will be difficult. The world's poor are already suffering from overpopulation, crowding, and food and water shortages, among other things. However, they are powerless and can do little to initiate change. The middle class does not yet feel the difficulties the poor live with, and if they did they would be limited in what they could do about them. Meaningful action depends on moving those who have power, and those people currently insulate themselves from the problems that the majority of us face.

Above all, we need to create new feedback mechanisms to replace the ones we destroyed when we overcame unpleasant controls, such as starvation and disease, on our once stable ecological niche. It is crucial that we utilize an effective feedback system that brings information about how we are harming the planet and what to do about it to those who hold power. An expanding group of concerned citizens demanding that the talents and knowledge of thinkers and scientific evidence be taken seriously and acted upon would push us closer to sustainability.

OTHER THINGS WE SHOULD DO

Every day, giving it virtually no thought, we are making a choice between destroying what nature has provided us with, or preserving the wonders around us for those who follow. Is allowing ignorance and our basic drives to govern us worth it? We can choose—those who follow us cannot! We need to do some important things now to understand our planet and ourselves.

What we need to know

What is the purpose for knowing anything? Essentially, there is just one purpose. Since life began on this planet, except for very recent human history, that purpose has been to further survival. Creatures knew what was needed to stay alive and procreate. Most knew little else. With us today, it is very different. We are swamped with information. We know a lot of things that have nothing to do with survival, and are ignorant of many things that are essential for it. Our knowledge and interests run off in other directions—sports, the lives of celebrities, the stock market, gossip, antiques, consumer products, the Civil War, wines, and opera. We read a lot of novels, watch TV, and do social networking. Some of this is good and necessary for our lives and our culture, however few of these things have anything to do with survival.

When life was simpler people were aware of what was going on around them, which was all that they needed to be aware of. Today we are immersed in huge quantities of information without an adequate instinct to pick out the essential. Where, for our own good and that of our species, should our interests lie today? Today, there is much we need to know—far more than at any time in the past. We need to know how to earn a living, manage our finances, raise a family, be good citizens, support our culture, and keep our species and planet healthy. Most of us do fairly well on the "earn a living" part, less well on the others, and miserably on the last. We simply cannot know all we should to live in this complex world, nonetheless we each do have a responsibility to society and our descendants to know what we can. As a species, we should be aware of and act on all things that bear on our survival.

Every day people, including political leaders, are making drastic changes to the world around us with little thought given to the consequences. While much is known about both the world and our brains, few people show more than a passing interest in these things, leaving such knowledge in books, journals, data banks, and the minds of a few people the rest of us ignore. What most of us do know is in unconnected packets, and is often wrong. As a species we could use our brains to overcome this predicament, but we do not.

We will look now at some things that all adults should have a basic awareness of, and better-educated people should know in greater detail.

We need to know how our brain works. To function effectively we need a rudimentary knowledge of how our brain, the tool we use in dealing with each other and our planet, works so we can overcome its deficiencies and use it to best advantage to better cope with problems that are rapidly growing in number, complexity, and gravity.

We cannot exchange our brains, but we can improve the way we use them. We can develop techniques and tools that supplement our brains, overcome their quirks, and enable us to do things we normally cannot. We already do this in many ways. We use writing to keep records, and telephones to talk farther than we can shout. We create organizations and tools to do things we as individuals and groups cannot do. Accounting, data banks, operations research, environmental impact studies, and orbiting satellites, when used effectively, can greatly extend our brain's capabilities. The scientific method, the systems approach, management systems, operations research, computers, brainstorming, and conflict resolution (formalized techniques for constructively resolving conflicts) expand the capacities of our minds. Finding and using more and better ways to do this, in addition to controlling or overriding certain primitive drives, should be a goal for all of us and something we expect from others.

We need to be made aware of our brain's weaknesses and limitations, so that we are modest about our abilities and ideas and are more open to possibilities to supplement and improve upon them. Although our ability to reason is limited, it is essential that we learn, and do our best, to think more clearly and resist having our thoughts manipulated by others such as charismatics and advertisers. Educators must help. This can be done. Ever since spending two weeks in primary school learning about propaganda and advertising, I have been conscious of mind manipulation and have resisted buying highly advertised products. It is also essential that educators do a far better job of helping their students to think rationally. Neurologist Michael Gazzaniga encourages us to do so. "...the quintessential human property of mind—rational processes—can occasionally override our more primitive beliefs. It isn't easy, but when it occurs, it represents our finest achievement."[53] Occasionally is not enough; we must strive to do it regularly.

We need to recognize our dependence on nature. It is essential that all of us understand how our planet works and what is threatening it—

ourselves. In our democracy we citizens, through the government representatives we elect, and by our lifestyles, are responsible for our effect on the well-being of other people and the planet we live on, now and in the future. We must recognize that we are dependent on nature, which maintains the remarkably narrow range of temperature and air pressure that is safe for us, provides us with necessities, and protects us from dangerous chemicals and radiation. Nature itself has limits to its ability to safely support the demands we place on it. We need to recognize what these limits are. A man sitting on the branch of a tree realizes it is important to him, so he will not cut it off. People who understand their dependence on nature and realize its fragility should be less likely to harm it. Unfortunately, there are few of us who understand this.

We need accurate information. For information to be used constructively, it needs to be right. Here the scientific method, where something must be tested repeatedly and evidence must be examined by one's peers, can help. Misinformation such as "climate change is not affected by human activity," promoted by political, religious, or other agendas, can bring on disaster. When we gain or use information we should be able to assume that it is correct. Nevertheless, at times it may be false, and we may even defend it and assure ourselves that it is right, because it coincides with our personal agenda.

We are dependent on the intent and knowledge of the providers of information such as schools and the media. Businesses inundate us with misleading information (mostly trivial images and brand names), and present us with ever more words and pictures, often in the form of entertainment, to gain our attention for presenting their messages. Advertisers and other parties wishing to influence our thinking have powerful resources to help them: access to much of our time, the effect of constant repetition, an understanding of what affects our beliefs and motivates us, and sophisticated techniques for manipulating our minds. They bypass our better selves and weak power of reason and appeal directly to our strong primitive instincts such as greed, fear, vanity, and our desire to please and impress our peers. Such information regularly crowds out what is more important for us to know.

We the public have been molded into dependable "consumers" to meet the needs of businesses expanding their markets. Our minds are continually being shaped by advertisers to want, want, want, which leads us to spend, spend, spend. Consequently a sizable amount of what we know and think about is in their hands. We know a lot about the qualities of a certain shampoo at the expense of what our survival on this planet depends on. Without understanding the outcome of our demands, we call for more and more of what pleases us. Educators and journalists must be expected to correctly inform us about our world, and encourage us to fill our minds with meaningful information instead of trivia and the irrelevant.

We need to recover our curiosity and get out of denial

Curiosity is a pathway to gaining much of the information we need. From my own observations I find that most people have very little curiosity about things related to how the real world works, or beyond the immediate future. In the past we didn't need that; it was only necessary to understand what went on in one's own vicinity and time. As I have already described, today our interests run off in many directions that have little to do with sustainability, but fail us on what does.

For information to be useful, it must be used. All too often not only lack of curiosity, but ignoring what we know, denial, and apathy stand in the way of information being used for the benefit of humanity and our planet. Too often facts do not arouse our limbic system, so we just ignore them. From my personal observations, many people just don't like to think much beyond their favorite subjects. It requires effort and the risk that we might learn things that challenge our beliefs; it is much easier to turn to the Internet or the TV than confront things that we would rather not know about or that might require a response.

There are critical issues we just do not think about, and few of us are even aware that we are ignoring them. For example, how will we feed people as our population grows and water and fertilizer become scarce? What will we do for energy when fossil fuels run out (if we haven't cooked ourselves first) and other forms of energy don't pan out?

A new mindset

We need a new mindset, a new way of looking at our relationship to each other and to the world. For most people reality is our own locality in the world, where we live right now. We need to understand and feel that the early twenty-first-century surroundings in which we live are a minute blip in human history and recognize that in this tiny instant we are now inflicting an explosion of burdens on our planet's life support system. We need to appreciate how unique our lives are in this brief moment of human history. How different our lives today are from those of just a century ago, and how different lives will be fifty years from now when all of the unsustainable activities we are engaged in bear fruit.

Having traveled and seen how most of the people on this planet live, I realize how uniquely privileged we who live comfortably are, and how our lives differ from those of the majority of people who share this planet with us. Our affluent island of human society is surrounded by immense expanses of people engulfed in misery and poverty. We must come to see that this is unjust and only getting worse. We need to empathize with distant peoples, and to decide to do what we can to help them. In becoming more than what we are, we must also recognize our moral obligation to leave those who follow us a healthy planet not depleted of nonrenewable resources.

Seeing time and our world this way makes me very conscious of my consumption and production of waste. If I were to eat a hamburger, I would likely think of the destruction of rain forests needed to produce the food to feed the animals, and the methane gas the animals produce. While reducing my part in this may seem to make little difference in what's happening, my awareness of it motivates me to think on a larger scale and do what I can to deal with our whole environmental situation. A widespread awareness of this would boost efforts to protect our planet.

See the big picture

It is essential that we look at the big picture, see our planet not as a collection of independent pieces, but rather as a single entity made up of components that interrelate and interact with one another and are changing by the day. Environmental and economic problems are never isolated but are part of a complex, interactive system originating in our past and extending into our future. In order to cope with the increasing complexity and the overload confronting us, we must develop effective new means for dealing with these things successfully. This will not be easy, as we have not done this in the past except in isolated instances. Considering what lies ahead, this must be done.

Get to causes

While it is important to deal with the most visible aspects of environmental problems, the ones that arouse most people, we cannot resolve our problems without dealing with the causes. To resolve our problems, people have to understand how exponential growth and the IPAT formula (Impact = Population × Affluence × Technology) work, and affect our planet's ability to support life, and that unending growth is impossible on a finite planet.

There are many problem areas where looking for and dealing with root causes can bear significant results. Incentives to waste and harm, such as subsidies for resource extraction and insulation from the harm caused by pollution, need to be eliminated. They should be replaced by taxes on carbon, for example, which would encourage conservation, reduce global warming, and reduce health problems caused by pollution. A tax on securities trading would discourage speculation, encourage individuals and groups that own shares in businesses to take a long-term interest in what they own, and be borne by those most able to pay. This would also help reduce economic inequality. While efforts to reduce the harmful side effects of our activities have been and are currently being made, they have to be intensified and the rationale behind them must be made clear to everyone.

Demand and respect honest science

Society must respect and demand clear thinking, verifiable information, and honest science. A very basic understanding of science, including how our world and minds work, should be up there with reading, writing, and arithmetic. All citizens should clearly understand what the scientific method is, and be wary of charlatans misleading them for their own benefit as carbon interests have been doing in order to put off action for dealing with climate change. Had science been taught as it should be taught, citizens would have a better understanding of what is happening to our planet, and what needs to be done to protect it. No one should teach science who does not have a love and understanding of it.

Recognize that at times there may be no good choices

Having broken out of our ecological niche, we have largely eliminated factors that maintained sustainability, such as population control by unpleasant means. We have avoided restoring controls on our place in nature and in our relationships with each other. To live sustainably on earth in peace we must impose restraints on ourselves that meet planetary needs. This will involve making compromises and sometimes unpleasant choices where there are none to our liking. At times reaching sustainability will require sacrifices, but we need to understand that the benefits far outweigh the costs.

Examine our beliefs

The world's people should make an overview of world beliefs and recognize the conflicts between them, and the human misery that has resulted from them in the past and still does today. We should all examine our own beliefs and look for the evidence that supports them and recognize the dangers of ill-founded beliefs such as that science is just another way of thinking. Where strong irrational beliefs persist, we must all work together to overcome the harm that they can cause.

Make better use of personality types

In order to effectively utilize individual abilities and society's potential to best advantage, it is imperative to turn to those most qualified, as I described in Chapter 5, for the tasks at hand. We must demand that "doers" turn to "thinkers" for an understanding of problems and tasks that need to be done.

Teachers, nurses, and plumbers need to pass examinations and be certified to do their jobs. Politicians do not. People who run for government office should be required to show their potential employers, the voters, their qualifications. Associations of economists, environmentalists, scientists, geographers, and historians could develop and give tests, the results of which would become public record. Besides testing the candidates, this would give these candidates an incentive to learn some things they badly need to know.

The inherent aggressiveness of many doers, the fact that they too often ignore the advice of thinkers, and their lack of understanding of complex problems will require education and strong controls to be sure their activities run along constructive lines. A major difficulty that must be overcome in the world's financial system is that those who can change it, who hold the power to do so, are those who most benefit from the status quo, and so are the least likely to bring about needed change.

Cooperate

I do not see how we can change ourselves genetically to behave on a higher moral level, however I hope that we are capable, at an intellectual level, of seeing the need to change the way we act. People have to understand that we are far better off working together than fighting, that cooperation produces benefits, and violence breeds harm and more and more violence. Nations and individuals must come to realize that much of the misery of the past could have been eliminated by cooperating and working together worldwide for the benefit of humanity and future generations, instead of each nation trying to come out on top. We all should understand how much we would benefit if the huge amounts of money spent on armaments could be used for education, much needed public infrastructure, and other sorely needed things.

We need a way to fill leadership positions with wise individuals who can lead and see the need for cooperation rather than competition, conflict, and winning—and see constructive results and reality as more important than pushing a political agenda and their own tenure in office. Drastically reducing the amount of money required by political campaigns would make it easier for candidates who recognize environmental problems and are willing to deal with them to run for office.

Replace our current economic system

We must replace our current economic system that calls for and depends on perpetual growth with one that promotes human well-being and sustainability. And, we need to discontinue using the Gross Domestic Product (GDP) indicator, which in addition to manufactured goods, includes the cost of producing and cleaning up pollution when measuring our economic health. We need a system that measures not just the economy, but environmental and human well-being, such as the Genuine Progress Indicator (GPI). GPI takes income distribution into account, along with household and volunteer work and the costs of natural, social, and human capital depletion.

In order to reach sustainability, we need to shrink our impact on our planet as represented by the IPAT formula. Doing this equitably will require sacrifices of a kind that few people in today's developed world are willing to make. We need to plan for this, and be determined to do whatever is necessary to protect the future of humankind and our planet. We have not yet started to think about how to accomplish this, but we must—and soon.

Evolve an environmental ethic

Albert Schweitzer proposed and adhered to a very simple ethic, "reverence for life." I can think of no better principle for individuals and governments to follow in dealing with one another and our planet. Valuing this and recognizing what really makes us happy, instead of many of the things we strive for—wealth, power, and status, for example—would make life better for everyone, and could form the basis of a just, workable, widely accepted ethical system.

Change our role models

Instead of admiring the rich and powerful, as many of us do, we should regularly remind ourselves that people obsessed with accumulating material goods are harming us all and that seekers of money and/or power are often limited people with primitive motives and warped outlooks on life. While some of those at the top are smart and talented, the only real talent of many is what is needed for gaining power or making money for themselves. If there was a wide acknowledgment of what these people really are, and recognition of the fact that their outrageous consumption, waste, and status-seeking harms us greatly, the public would see those promoting unnecessary consumption as limited, unpatriotic Earthlings. This would make those goals less attractive.

If society attached a stigma to occupations, activities, and individuals that hurt us and raised the status of those that benefit us, more of us would turn to socially useful occupations, and politicians and businesspeople would be motivated to behave more constructively.

Happiness and Real Income per Capita in the United States 1972-2008

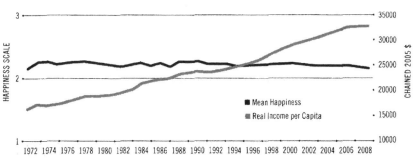

Figure 25. Mean happiness (the darker of the two lines on the graph above) is the average reply from respondents to the U.S. General Social Survey. The survey question asks: "Taken all together, how would you say things are these days? Would you say that you are not too happy, pretty happy or very happy?" These values were coded as 1, 2 and 3, respectively.[55] Source: General Social Survey data available at *http://www.norc.org/GSS+Website*. Real income per capita based on the author's calculation using data from the Bureau of Economic Analysis and the Census Bureau.

Achieve real happiness

A number of research projects have shown that once basic needs such as food, clothing, shelter, medical care, satisfying personal relationships, and a meaningful way to spend one's time have been filled, the accumulation of additional money does not increase happiness.[54] Widespread recognition of this would encourage people to live in peace with one other and our planet.

Chapter Seven

OPPORTUNITIES FOR THE COMMITTED

Although our situation may appear hopeless, it is not

After looking at all of the subjects I have covered, one could view our situation as hopeless. Unless we have passed a tipping point, it is not. While we cannot in our lifetimes or those of our grandchildren have the kind of biosphere people had a hundred years ago, by taking action soon we can do a lot to mitigate what is now threatening our future. If we halt the downward spiral we are now in by significantly reducing the burdens we are placing on the world, stop waging war on each other, share resources equitably, and recognize what really makes us happy, a smaller population can lead rewarding, enjoyable lives on Earth far into the future.

The hope of change rests on the already committed

While needs and opportunities to improve our situation are widespread, I will confine my discussion here to what environment-minded people can do, and things that have to do with how we deal with our planet.

I have listed things that need to be done and dealt with, but the likelihood of these things happening to a meaningful extent is not good at this time. The relatively small number of people concerned about how we deal with the planet *will* understand the great need to do these things, however the mass of humanity and its leaders will largely ignore them or at most make inadequate efforts to deal with them. So the burden of instigating significant change rests on the few who see the gravity of our situation and are deeply committed to doing something about it.

There are others, also concerned, who think that we are on the way to resolving our problems through constructing wind turbines and solar collectors, recycling, protecting whales, and the like. Others yet recognize that there are environmental problems, but continue to drive their SUVs

...and otherwise live as they always have. Increasing the strength and efficacy of the environmental movement rests on the shoulders of the first group, those who see the seriousness of our situation and are already actively engaged.

Difficult as it is to see the problems before us clearly and their potential solutions, it is even more difficult to achieve those solutions, especially when the effort is being spearheaded by a limited group of individuals already like Sisyphus working against great odds. But it must be done. They need to find more effective ways to arouse the rest of us. In doing so, to conserve and focus their energy, it would be well to keep Reinhold Niebuhr's serenity prayer in mind. "God, give us grace to accept with serenity the things that cannot be changed, courage to change the things which should be changed, and the wisdom to distinguish the one from the other."

Just by joining and/or supporting groups like the Sierra Club, the Audubon Society, 350.org, or the Center for the Advancement of the Steady State Economy, and actively participating in and supporting their activities, concerned individuals can strengthen the environmental movement. Getting their friends involved or volunteering for one of them will do even more.

Improve effectiveness by working together

Environmentalists and environmental groups need to recognize that the root cause of their individual concerns, the impending extinction of polar bears, future water shortages, and climate change, for example, is human Population multiplied by individual Affluence, modified by how Technology is used, as summarized by the IPAT formula. By looking for the origins of specific environmental problems, they would see that just about all of them can be explained by this formula. By recognizing this and publicly proclaiming it—as often as possible—they could more effectively aid their individual goals. Forming a worldwide association of environmentally concerned organizations would help them all pursue their causes and strengthen the whole environmental movement. Environmentalists constructively working together in this way worldwide would be a responsible alternative to the shameful example of world political leaders focusing on narrow national interests, disregarding the overall good of humanity and our planet.

In their current weak position, environmentalists have little effect on who runs governments. Nonetheless, they can prepare the ground for the time it becomes possible to deal with this problem. Inspiration can be found in the group of professors at Freiburg University in Germany opposed to the Nazis known as the Freiburg Circle. The group was made up of economists at the university led by Adolf Lampe, the husband of a distant relative of mine. Meeting in secrecy in the dark days of the Third Reich, they formulated a postwar economic program, the Social Market Economy (*Sozialen Marktwirtschaft*), which played a major role in the German economic recovery after 1945. Although my relative's husband, Adolf Lampe, died in 1946, the result of torture by the Gestapo, Konrad Adenauer, the first postwar chancellor of Germany, and Ludwig Erhard, his Minister of Economics, carried out the group's plan, which led to the German "*Wirtschaftswunder*" (Economic Miracle) in the years that followed. Today, environmentalists can discuss possibilities among themselves, write articles and books, use the Internet in every way they can, and have conferences. They should devise and publicly propose alternatives to what governments are currently doing and how tax systems function. This work today would provide the spark that could make widespread discussion and action on this subject possible in the future, and lead the world to better informed, cooperative, more forward-thinking leadership.

Applying economic pressure by divesting funds and boycotting have become effective tools for bringing about change; they have worked with apartheid in South Africa, for example. Agreeing on everything may not always be possible for all groups seeking to protect the environment and/or establish greater justice and equity between people, nevertheless an organized global environmental movement utilizing these tools would have some direct global impact, and in addition draw attention to businesses significantly contributing to environmental problems such as Exxon and McDonald's. These companies would not like the orchestrated publicity they would get from such campaigns. An easy way for individuals to divest is to transfer their assets to an ethically responsible investment fund.

Learning from the advertising business and political campaigns, in a unified effort environmentalists around the world should repeatedly point out the obvious to the public, such as the fact that unending economic growth is an oxymoron that can only lead to catastrophe, and that we are already overpopulated and must work to restrain population growth and then reverse it.

An organized environmental movement would present opportunities that individual groups do not have to draw world attention to critical situations and present solutions. For example, a world conference on human well-being and happiness backed by all environmentalists and their organizations would be difficult for the world media and politicians to ignore. I believe that other organizations and individuals would eagerly join in to support this. Critical topics could be addressed by well-known, respected individuals. Personalities such as Ban Ki-moon, Pope Francis, the Dalai Lama, and the King of Bhutan should see this as an opportunity to present their thoughts to the world. Other important thinkers and theologians of all religions could also be asked to participate. The problems of greed for power and wealth, and unwavering national interests over world welfare could be discussed by highly respected psychiatrists, psychologists, neurologists, and neuroscientists, as well as ethicists and theologians. The questions of what brings real happiness and why unlimited economic growth cannot work on a finite planet would comprise an important part of such an event.

The newly formed environmental movement should urge members who belong to professional organizations of psychologists and psychiatrists to get these groups to hold events discussing the motivations that drive people to strive for positions of wealth and power that have nothing to do with real human happiness. Results of such investigations should be published widely and brought before the public, so that it can see these individuals for what they really are.

Create a new milieu

Today the American public is constantly bombarded with the idea that the free market and perpetual economic growth are essential to create jobs and resolve our economic problems. This has established a public mindset that needs to be challenged and changed. Repeatedly presenting easy-to-understand, irrefutable reasons why pursuing these goals is dangerous in today's environmentally threatened world can make it clear that this is not working, and is taking us on a road to serious trouble. Environmentalists need to make it clear to the public that unlimited population and economic growth are simply impossible in a limited space. They must also demand alternative ways to manage the economy, point out specific cases of irrational thinking, and insist that governments, the media, and the public look for root causes and connections.

International cooperation does not come easy to many of the highly ambitious individuals who hold positions of power. However, cooperation and accommodation are essential for dealing with climate change preservation of life in the world's oceans. Making the truth of the and the limitations of our planet clear to most people, and learni the advertising industry again by repeating them strongly and : should help lead to a new milieu based on reality. It would also provide a receptive setting for environmentalists to present their individual causes in—as well as further world peace. The environmental movement should keep pounding home the facts that to resolve our problems we need to look at the whole, see time as ongoing rather than just the few years ahead, and be mindful of our responsibility to those who follow us.

Press for replacing the GDP indicator

Events such as the United Nations summit for the adoption of the post-2015 development agenda to improve global well-being present an opportunity for environmentalists to present critical ideas to the world public. For example: 1. Relying on economic growth to solve all our economic problems is a road to catastrophe; 2. Using the Gross Domestic Product indicator (which includes the costs of producing environmental damage, cleaning it up and the medical problems resulting from it, etc.) as a goal for human well-being is both nonsensical and dangerous; 3. Evidence shows that accumulating more money and goods beyond a point does not increase happiness.

Organizing a worldwide conference of notable environmentalists and sympathetic economists calling for a replacement for the GDP as an indicator would provide a tempting feast of subjects for the media, encourage public discussion, and get people to think. It is probably too late for world environmentalists to set up an umbrella organization and organize a conference before the UN's goals are set in 2015, nevertheless there is an opportunity here to present rational, indisputable ideas that should not be missed. Sensible alternatives to the GDP have been presented and should be looked at, for example: the Genuine Progress Indicator (GPI); the Index of Sustainable Economic Welfare (ISEW); and the Kingdom of Bhutan's goal to achieve Gross National Happiness (GNH).

Spread the word

While the widespread organization of the environmental movement is taking place, there are other things that can be done. The movement can expand its impact by awakening and gaining support from those who mistakenly believe we are now on the path to sustainability, and hopefully from some of the now blasé drivers of SUVs. The already committed must help these other groups understand that our earth is changing by the day, that conditions are rapidly growing worse without a clear end in sight, and that this can be reversed. As the milieu among the well-educated changes, the task of arousal will become easier and gain support. The backing of these new converts to participation would add significant power to the environmental movement.

With their help, we need to do all we can in our contacts with open-minded people to discuss environmental issues, foster clear thinking on largely ignored, easily understood ideas, draw their attention to our ecological footprints, and suggest reliable sources of information. Many environmentally concerned individuals like myself learn and think about various problems, but fail to develop the skills needed to persuade and arouse others. Becoming good at this could be a real boost to the environmental movement. There are numerous books dealing with persuasion that can help us, including *Words That Work: It's Not What You Say, It's What People Hear,* by Frank Luntz, and various books by George Lakoff on framing. We should also encourage people to require evidence rather than blindly follow an agenda. Environmentalists should have effective answers ready for the inevitable questions. To arouse and inspire others, we need to be prepared to speak to their emotions as well as their intellects. We should encourage those who develop an awareness of and concern for our current situation to join in and support environmental organizations they see as important, and to visit their websites and join their blogs.

Reaching out like this can be awkward and uncomfortable at times. Wishing to retain relationships, in the past I was shy about doing this. Now that I recognize the importance of educating others, however, I carefully choose promising subjects, risk rejection, and do my best to educate people without turning them off.

Today there are many groups and individuals setting examples of how we should live, but they are not having the impact on society that they should. Good real-life examples can be powerful motivators. A widespread understanding by environmentalists of the possibilities here, and a serious effort by them to utilize this potential could influence many. For such an effort to be effective it would be important that people notice and understand the reasons behind what participants do and recognize their commitment. These efforts would have to be carefully orchestrated so that people would be moved by the dedication of the participants, and not view them as extremists or crazies.

There are many ways for environmentalists to openly demonstrate their awareness of the dangers we face and show their resolve to do what they can to mitigate them. Where we choose to live, how we move about, what we eat and wear, and how we care for what we own can show our commitment to reducing the burdens we place on our planet. Here's an example of what I see as a bad choice. A well-known environmental organization that used to hold its meetings at a central location in Cincinnati moved them to a remote suburban location requiring extensive driving. By doing so, it may have reduced driving for members who had moved out to that area, but it missed an opportunity to demonstrate its opposition to suburban sprawl. This is not the kind of example such an organization should present. Environmental activists should look across the board for opportunities where they can set positive examples, and make it clear to others why they do what they do.

Environmentalists wishing to devote themselves full-time for a period of months or years to pushing the broad or a limited environmental agenda could join yet to be established groups in some ways resembling Catholic or Buddhist monastic orders. This would give interested individuals opportunities to connect to organized, promising organizations with a clear programs and techniques for expanding public awareness of the dangers we face and offering possible solutions. It would also enable them to concentrate on, and devote themselves full-time to the cause. Such groups would offer them support from like-minded individuals. The differences between such groups, such as how and where they work, would offer potential participants a broad range of opportunities.

A STRONGER ENVIRONMENTAL MOVEMENT OFFERS OTHER OPPORTUNITIES

Work within our own religious communities

Religion is a powerful force in the world. Large numbers of environmentally concerned individuals belong to organized religious groups, and herein lies opportunity. While some groups ignore or see environmental problems as irrelevant, many have taken environmental problems seriously and recognized their responsibility towards the planet. They have made statements and organized conferences; nevertheless they can do better. Environmentally concerned members of these organizations have an opportunity to see that they do.

An umbrella group of environmentally oriented organizations would make it easy for members and supporters of different groups, the Audubon Society, the World Wildlife Fund, and the Nature Conservancy, for example, within a particular religious denomination to connect with each other. Working together they would have a voice that would be hard to ignore and that top leaders of their religious organizations would want to listen to. They could press their religious group and individual congregations to vigorously express their concerns about the environment, and have them take strong positions on issues such as global warming and excessive consumption. Responsibilities towards our environment should be a regular topic in sermons and study groups. These kinds of actions would have an impact on many religious people, and consequently the behavior of governments.

Educate journalists

Journalists are a vital bridge between reality, the public, and politicians. To do their job properly, they need to understand some fundamental things about science and be able to present a clear picture of reality to their audience. Working together, environmental groups could plan and present workshops with noted speakers directed to journalists and editors. These would broaden their knowledge on the basics and breadth of environmental problems and their root causes, and make sure that all attendees understand that science is not just another agenda, but an honest search for evidence and truth. People in the media must also be shown that presenting a knowledgeable expert paired with someone representing a special interest is not "balanced reporting," but misleading, and therefore bad journalism. As more attention is given to climate change and other environmental problems in the media, many journalists, beyond members of the Society of Environmental Journalists (I am a member because I think their work is essential) might be eager to attend such workshops. Foundations interested in the environment would see the value in having better-informed journalists committed to passing accurate information about the environment on to their audience. They should be willing to fund such workshops generously.

Get scientists to speak up and educators to teach real science

Honest, informed scientists spend their time searching for reality without being influenced by ideologies. The public needs to understand this simple fact. Many scientists work in areas related to our environment and understand what is happening today. There is a tremendous amount of knowledge and brainpower out there that needs to speak up, like James Hansen who resigned his position as the head of the NASA Goddard Institute for Space Studies in New York City in order to take a more active role in the political and legal efforts to limit greenhouse gases. Already in his seventies, his arrests for protesting the TransCanada pipeline have drawn considerable attention. More scientists standing up, speaking out, and taking risks would help many people become more aware of the grim reality we are headed for. Environmentalists should find and encourage more scientists to do this.

Just as creationists have run for school boards, environmentalists should do the same and make sure that real science is taught in classrooms. An organized environmental movement would make this easier. Environmentalists involved with science should build bonds with colleges and individuals who educate teachers, and do all they can to see that those who teach science to young people truly understand what science is. Where possible environmentalists should participate in workshops for teachers.

Push important business leaders to broaden their concerns

Many of the rich and CEOs of major corporations live in a limited, narrow world of their own making which includes people who think like they do and generally tell them what they want to hear, and excludes individuals who could broaden their outlook and tell them things they ought to know. If business leaders were to hear the truth about our situation from respected scientists in an attractive setting like an exclusive meeting for influential decision-makers, some of them might gain an understanding of the seriousness of the situation we are facing, and see the need for change. Organizing a group of important, well-known scientists, including Nobel Laureates, to present a one-day workshop, and with considerable publicity inviting important business leaders to it, would make it awkward for them to decline. Having some move to the side of the environmental movement would be a significant boost for dealing with what we face.

Get artists and other specialists to help

Today many visual artists seem to be more interested in form than in intellectual content, leaving a void in social commentary. We should make a concerted effort to reach out to and encourage painters, sculptors, photographers, poets, novelists, cartoonists, composers, lyricists, and choreographers to depict environmental and social problems and show how our greed, ignorance, irrationality, and fallacious beliefs contribute to them. Artists should grasp opportunities to expose contemporary bad behavior, ignorance, and apathy, and express their own feelings and thinking regarding ways to meet the need for a better world. Honoré Daumier and Diego Rivera, and works such as *A Modest Proposal, Oliver Twist, The Three Penny Opera* and *Animal Farm* have done this in the past. As I write this, *Silent Night,* a powerful opera with music composed by Kevin Puts with libretto by Mark Campbell, is being performed by a number of opera companies in this country. It beautifully demonstrates the stupidity of war and the benefits of cooperation. Stories and metaphors can arouse an important part of our brain that facts and figures cannot. Information and data can leave us unmoved, but artists through their craft can give us a feel for where we are, where we are headed, and where we might go instead.

Uri Hasson, assistant professor at Princeton University's Department of Psychology and the Neuroscience Institute, uses MRI machines to ob-

Figure 26. "The Legislative Belly," political commentary by Honoré Daumier. The Brooklyn Museum, Ella W. Woodward Memorial Fund

serve the effect of stories on the brain. He discovered that "Stories have a very strong impact on the brain. They're very strong stimuli that can take control over the listener's brain."[56] To encourage small families, the Population Media Center of Shelburne, Vermont, uses serialized dramas on radio and television in Third World countries where characters evolve into role models for the audience to foster positive behavior change. Followup studies have shown significant reductions in family size and in the spread of AIDS among the audiences of these programs. This success needs to be extended into other media. Utilizing the power of stories, writers should be encouraged to produce novels, short stories, poems, plays, and movie scripts to develop an awareness of threats to our planet and promote solutions, as well as encourage cooperative, peaceful behavior.

We should encourage individuals with special knowledge in environmental areas—ecology, energy, or oceanography for example—to volunteer to teach adult education classes at universities and colleges near where they live. As news coverage of environmental problems increases, there should be a growing demand for such courses.

Environmentalists and individuals promoting world peace and cooperation should encourage psychologists, psychiatrists, neuroscientists, and anthropologists to write popular books and articles on the minds of despots and greedy people. Discussing and dissecting what drives them and allows them to behave as they do should intellectually strip them before the public and affect their self-esteem and position as status symbols.

Stage dramatic events

A dramatic event can get people thinking. In January 1971 I attended a talk about air pollution in Cincinnati. It was growing worse, and not enough was being done about it. During the talk I wondered how to get people to think about what pollution and automobile traffic would be like in the future if we continued as we were. During the question and answer period I asked if anyone there would help me work on a demonstration of what would happen if we let things get worse. A mass "drive-in" to Washington, DC, and Detroit of concerned individuals from across the nation on April 2 would show what lay ahead. A reporter called me a week later to see how my plans were going. There were none, because no one had volunteered to join me in this. Thinking quickly, I told him to call back in a couple of days. He did and I had cooked up a good story for him. The telephone next to my bed started ringing at five a.m. the next morning, first a call from the *Detroit Free Press* followed by other newspapers and radio stations. Letters to editors flowed in, often quite hostile, several calling me a communist. Sadly, some people didn't get the point, although it should have gotten many people to think of what cities would be like, jammed with automobiles. Considering the harm such an event could cause by preventing emergency vehicles from getting through, I abandoned my plans well before April 2. Environmentalists should look for opportunities, dramatic or otherwise, to wake people up and get them thinking about what lies ahead of us.

Find other ways to dramatize important issues

Some years ago, without success, I tried to interest a number of organizations and individuals in creating a war museum that would show the brutality of war rather than glorifying it. Well done, such a museum could have a powerful impact on people. A group of organizations promoting this idea together would have significantly more effect than I did.

Help others to recognize what we are

Recognizing that we have not evolved sufficiently to consistently function safely in the civilization we now have, and deciding to do something about it, will enable us to better understand our predicament. Then we can move beyond our current inadequate efforts and deal effectively with our complex problems. But how to get there from where we are? We need to think about this. Here is an idea that could help. Organizing, running, and publicizing conferences with notable scholars in areas like anthropology and evolutionary psychology to discuss this problem would draw attention to it and get people thinking.

Because facing our inadequacies could be seen as humiliating, developing such an awareness will be difficult. There will be strong resistance, including from many religious and some political groups. Although our shortcomings should be clear to anyone who looks at evidence and sees how we treat our planet and one another, some people will hate us for pointing this out. The stakes are high, so we must do this carefully so as not to offend, and when it is unavoidable bear the hate. Such an awareness, if it can be developed, would create greater modesty and willingness to examine our own behavior. Although this will be difficult to achieve, the environmental movement would be given a significant lift by it.

Figure 27. Mormon missionaries. Photo by Jeff Blake, Getty Images

WE NEED *YOUR* SUGGESTIONS

I have offered some suggestions here, but motivating and organizing people is not my strength. Fortunately there are people who understand our problem and can develop strategies to work on this. Hopefully, some will come up with ideas that can motivate significant numbers of people to become actively engaged before we reach an environmental Pearl Harbor too late in the game.

Erik Assadourian of the Worldwatch Institute is one such person who offers some interesting examples in his chapter titled, "Reengineering Cultures to Create a Sustainable Civilization," in the important State of the World 2013 book, *Is Sustainability Still Possible?*[57] Among the things he suggests is the development of an evangelical "Eco-Philosophy." He mentions various religious groups, and how among them every year more than fifty thousand young Mormons fan out around the world as missionaries contacting people one-on-one with significant success. The success of these groups and their techniques can serve as models for environmentalists. Organized groups proselytizing for the environment could provide individuals an opportunity to become active and work for a better world. Their commitment and dedication would move many people to take our environmental problems seriously.

IN CONCLUSION

It is hard to tell a story without a pleasing ending. The way many people think today, the future will just get better, and those who throw cold water on this euphoria are, as I have experienced myself, to be avoided. Piercing illusions may not make one popular, but ignoring unpleasant realities paves the way to disaster.

What I have written about here is what I observe from my corner of this world and have read about. I am neither an anthropologist nor an evolutionary psychologist. I just point out trends, and make no predictions, except the most inevitable, and then in general terms. I look at the broad picture that includes the interactions of environmental problems, and the parts we play in this. I am sure that other people must have come to the same conclusion that I have, simply that humanity has not evolved enough to live safely in this new world we have created—unless we consciously manage to move beyond what we now are.

I hope that you who read this will come up with better ideas than those presented here. And I will be grateful to those who show me that my view of our situation is overly pessimistic or faulty. I hope that along with the limited but crucial efforts we are already making to protect our planet, new ideas on how to overcome the obstacles I have described will be able to guide us off the path to devastation and on to sustainability. Then when I gaze out from my thirteenth-floor balcony, there will be something to smile about.

PART TWO

∾

Our Planet Today

by

Gary Gardner

INTRODUCTION

Environmental degradation and resource depletion are accelerating rapidly, and the results are felt even at a global level. But depletion and degradation are often imperceptible in daily life; many people today are only dimly aware of rapidly developing environmental trends and their effect on the world. Having lived through many decades of degradation with little apparent damage to our prospects for a good life (at least in wealthy countries), we humans are often complacent in the face of growing risks to our planet and its people.

This part of the book was developed to demonstrate the unusual and urgent nature of this moment in history. For each issue discussed, we document how our current era is different from previous ones. We show how rapidly trends are unfolding. And we explain why this period of rapid change matters, for the planet and for the people it supports.

We will look at nine essential areas of concern. The first two, population growth and consumption growth, are powerful drivers of all the others. Their importance was stated elegantly in a helpful formula developed by Paul Ehrlich and John Holdren in the 1970s for analyzing environmental impact: Impact is a function of Population, Affluence, and Technology, or in brief, I=PAT. As more people inhabit our planet, as they become wealthier, and as their technological prowess grows, the impact on the environment generally increases. Of course, the impact of these variables is not preordained. Technology sometimes reduces environmental impact and affluence can be achieved with a light environmental footprint. But in general, as P, A, and T have increased over the last century and more, environmental impact has increased as well.

Thus the series of sustainability issues begins with two key drivers of environmental outcomes and sources of unsustainable economic activity, population and consumption growth. (Technology is not covered here because of the lack of an overarching indicator to measure its impact.) We will then turn to the Ecological Footprint for a global assessment of the effect of human activities on the natural world. This is followed by a review of five areas, from food and cropland to climate, that are vital for the creation of sustainable economies. Finally, this section of the book closes on a note of hope, by suggesting an alternative vision for economies, based on stabilized population and consumption levels.

TABLE OF CONTENTS

POPULATION

Growth in human population sets the past century apart from all previous human history. Before 1900, no human generations had seen increases in human population like the ones experienced between 1900 and 2013, when the human family increased nearly fivefold.[1] The tremendous acceleration of human population growth is sometimes illustrated by showing the quickening pace at which population has reached various billion-person landmarks. That perspective is reflected in Table A-1.

For thousands of human generations who lived as hunter-gatherers or in small villages or towns, the idea of a billion-person world would have seemed fantastical. By contrast, the generation born just before 1927—today's eighty-seven-year-olds and those older—has lived through *five sep-*

Table A-1. Global Population Landmarks

	Global Population Landmark (billion persons)	Year Landmark Reached	Years to Reach Landmark
Historical	1	1804	Tens of thousands
	2	1927	123
	3	1960	33
	4	1974	14
	5	1987	13
	6	1999	12
	7	2011	12
Future	8	~2025	14
	9	~2040	15
	10	~2060	20

Source: United Nations

Figure A-2. Global Population Growth, Developing and Developed Countries

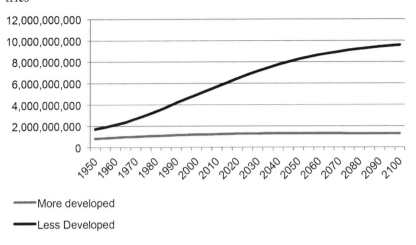

More developed

Less Developed

arate billion-person additions to the global population, an unprecedented demographic acceleration. Indeed, most of us experience today's rapid population growth as yawningly normal: we hardly notice that humanity compresses into about a decade the same population increase that occurred between the Stone Age and the Industrial Revolution.

Table A-1 also shows that global population growth has begun to slow a bit, and the period between billion-person additions is projected to lengthen slightly in the decades ahead. But the locomotive-like momentum of population growth means that more billions are likely to be added before global population stabilizes: humans number 7.1 billion in 2014 but are projected to reach ten billion around 2060, and the United Nations does not project a peak in global population until after 2100. [2] (Data cited here are based on the UN's "medium variant" projections, a middle estimate of population growth.)

While the global trend is strongly upward for decades ahead, most of this growth will occur in developing countries as improvements in public health lower mortality rates there. (See Figure A-2.) Already, ninety-five percent of the global increase in population occurs in developing countries, and this share is projected to grow over the rest of the century. By contrast, some industrial nations—Japan, Russia, and Germany are the largest of these—have recently begun to shrink in population, and China, the world's most populous country, is projected to see its population peak by around 2030, then start to contract.[3] But growth in the developing world—again, largely because of a welcome decrease in mortality rates— is likely to more than offset these notable declines, which is why global population continues to surge upward.

DRIVERS OF POPULATION CHANGE

Population growth (or decline) is a complex process, but globally it can be summarized as the outcome of two dueling pressures: birth rates and death rates. (At the national level—or at any other sub-global level—growth rates are also affected by migration.) If birth rates dominate, global population will increase; if death rates dominate, global population declines. For thousands of years, most societies endured high rates of death, and had high rates of birth. The nearly offsetting birth and death rates produced very slow growth in population for thousands of years— so slow that one to five thousand years were typically needed for global population to double. By contrast, in the twentieth century global population doubled from three billion to six billion in just thirty-nine years.

As nations urbanized and industrialized over time, they invested in clean water, sewage disposal, medical advances, and food production, all of which improved health and reduced death rates—while birth rates remained at previous levels. The result was rapidly growing populations. (Many developing countries today are in this category: death rates are falling as public health measures conquer diseases from cholera to whooping cough, but birth rates have not yet slowed or are only beginning to slow.) As economies prospered further, a new demographic phase emerged in which death rates continued to decline, but birth rates also declined as contraceptive technologies improved and became more available worldwide and parents took greater control of decisions regarding family size. In addition, urbanization, with requirements for education and limits to the usefulness of childhood labor, increased the cost of having children.

Thus the pattern that characterizes this moment in human history is one of rapid increases in national populations before they stabilize and eventually fall, due to changes in important social and economic variables. Population projections for the rest of the century are based on the assumption that the pattern that characterizes the past will apply to the future as well.

Demography is much more than a numbers game: the social and economic variables that drive changes in population—including investments in public health, access to education and health care, and the extent of women's empowerment—translate to real changes in people's well-being. And changes in well-being, in turn, affect population growth.

The community of nations is making strong (though inadequate) efforts to reduce various dimensions of poverty, some of which could affect population growth. The Millennium Development Goals, objectives set by the United Nations for elimination of the most severe forms of human deprivation by 2015, have spurred action to reduce the number of people living in extreme poverty and to cut in half the proportion of people without access to sanitary sources of drinking water. [4] And major gains have been made in the fight against malaria and tuberculosis. [5] Success in these areas could reduce death rates and therefore increase population pressure initially, but they are also likely to lay the groundwork for the economic and social stability that reduces birth rates and slows population growth.

To be sure, suffering is still widespread: some 870 million people, roughly one in eight humans, live with chronic hunger, and some 2.8 billion people lack access to adequate sanitation, a major public health problem that contributes to increased death rates. [6] And six million children still die each year before reaching their fifth birthday. [7]

Meanwhile, the wealthiest in the world are extraordinarily rich. Credit Suisse's World Wealth Report 2013 reveals that more than two-thirds of the global population controls just three percent of global wealth, while the world's richest 0.7 percent of population controls forty-one percent of the world's wealth.[8] (See Table A-3.) Oxfam puts the numbers a different way,

Table A-3. The concentration of global wealth

Household wealth	Share of world population in %	Share of world wealth in %
Less than $10,000	68.7	3.0
$10,000 - $100,000	22.9	13.7
$100,000 - $1 million	7.7	42.3
More than $1 million	0.7	41.0

Source: See endnote [11]

reporting in 2014 that the richest eighty-five people in the world have as much wealth as the poorest *half* of the world population, more than three billion people.[9] And in all of the high-income G20, the world's wealthiest twenty countries, except for South Korea, inequality continues to increase.[10]

Much work remains to be done before all people will have a decent shot at a dignified life. Achieving social and economic stability will be a major contribution to dignified lives and stable populations.

GROWING POPULATION, FIXED RESOURCES

Global population growth occurs in a world of fixed resources—including nonrenewables like minerals and fuels, and renewables such as forests and water—resulting in an ongoing decline in resources per person. While many resources are quite plentiful, critical resources such as water, farmland, and oil are increasingly scarce, while natural services such as pollution absorption are increasingly impaired. The loss or degradation of these resources has already begun to limit possibilities for sustainable development in some countries.

A few resources that show signs of short supply are summarized below and elaborated on in later sections.

Water resources—The United Nations estimates that 1.8 billion people will live with absolute water scarcity (fewer than 500 cubic meters per person) by 2025, and that two-thirds of the world will be living under water-stressed conditions.[12] Water scarcity is already limiting agricultural production in the Middle East and North Africa, and possibly China, and may soon do so in India and the United States. Meanwhile, seven major river basins, including the Nile, the Indus, the Colorado, and the Yellow River basins were identified in 2013 as closed or closing, meaning that present allocations of water are so great that no additional allocations can be made without depriving river ecology of the water it needs.[13]

Agriculture—Agricultural land, and water for agriculture, are in increasingly short supply in many countries. Irrigated area per person is declining, putting pressure on farmers and scientists to produce more on a shrinking agricultural endowment, even as demand for agricultural output is projected to increase by sixty percent between 2005/07 and 2050.[14] Meanwhile, major fisheries in the world's oceans have been fished to exhaustion, leading fishers to rely on aquaculture to meet global demand. Adding two to three billion more people to the human family this century will make providing food for all in a world of constrained agriculture much more difficult.

Atmosphere—Factories, cars and farms, fueled by demand from growing and more prosperous societies, continue to emit growing quantities of greenhouse gases. But the capacity of our planet's atmosphere to absorb greenhouse gases is fixed, so emissions accumulate, trap heat, and change the planet's climate. The international panel of scientists charged with studying climate is set to issue a new set of findings that describe the situation in increasingly dire terms as average global temperature is on track to shoot well past the two-degree warming threshold that scientists have warned should not be surpassed.

Biodiversity—Greater numbers of people, and the economic activity they engage in, have taken a serious toll on the web of life on the planet. According to the International Union for the Conservation of Nature, twenty-five percent of the world's mammal species, thirteen percent of birds, and forty-one percent of amphibians are threatened with extinction.[15] Meanwhile, the capacity of nature to provide important economic services, from pollination of crops to flood control and erosion prevention, is degraded in many regions as natural systems are damaged by human activities. A 2010 study of thirty-one indicators related to biodiversity found that all indicators of the state of biodiversity such as extent of habitat were in decline, while indicators of pressure on biodiversity such as alien species and nitrogen pollution were all increasing—despite a 2002 commitment by world leaders to reduce significantly the rate of biodiversity loss.[16]

FURTHER EXPLORATION

Royal Society, "People and the Planet" (London: Royal Society, April 2012)

Alan Weisman, *Countdown: Our Last Best Hope for a Future on Earth* (New York: Little, Brown, and Company, 2013)

The Millennium Development Goals Report 2013, (New York: United Nations, 2013)

Credit Suisse Research Institute, "World Wealth Report 2013" (Zurich: Credit Suisse AG, October 2013)

CONSUMPTION

Consumption is a major driver of economic activity: some sixty percent of the gross domestic product (GDP) of the world's economies consists of consumer spending on goods and services.[17] Consumption is also a major source of environmental and resource decline. It leads to more mining, drilling, farming, fishing, and logging; more refining, pulping, husking, and other processing; more manufacturing, assembly, and transport; and after goods and services are consumed, more disposal in landfills or incinerators. Its outsize role in stimulating economic activity and generating pollution is what earns consumption a leading place (along with population growth and technological advance) as a source of environmental impact.

Consumption is driven in part by population growth (more people means more consumption), but also by greater prosperity, which typically drives up consumption per person. As population growth expands the ranks of consumers globally, and as each person consumes more as a result of greater prosperity, overall consumption, and its impact on the environment, tends to increase as well.

As long as economies are built on a linear flow of materials—meaning that resources are typically used once, then discarded—continued economic growth will spell increased depletion of resources and degradation of ecosystems. The alternative is to create "circular economies" in which waste is largely unknown, where recycling, reuse, and remanufacturing is the norm; and where "dematerialization" is achieved to the maximum extent possible (through, for example, the use of services such as car-sharing, to replace goods such as private cars). Sustainable consumption will also involve a greater appreciation for living simply, and for maximizing quality of life over high levels of material consumption.

PROJECTED CONSUMPTION

Consumption at the global level is growing in step with rapid economic growth in many emerging industrial economies. Because many of these countries are still building infrastructure, their resource use is not just to meet household consumer demand, but also to construct roads, buildings, water and sewage systems, airports, power grids, irrigation canals, railroads, and other works that require enormous volumes of energy, metals, minerals, wood, water, biomass, and other materials. Today's increase in economic demand and resource use is huge: analysts at the McKinsey Global Institute note that China and India alone "are experiencing roughly ten times the economic acceleration of the Industrial Revolution, on 100 times the scale"—because of their far larger populations—"resulting in an economic force that is 1000 times as big."[18]

The trend is projected to continue into the future. World GDP is estimated to be more than four times larger in 2050 than it was in 2007.[19] At least 150 million people will be entering the middle class each year through 2030, raising the middle class share of global population to almost sixty percent. Much of this prosperity will take place in today's emerging economies: China's economy is expected to overtake that of the US by 2025, and most emerging market economies are projected to be larger than that of the UK by 2050.[20]

Of course, consumption of resources is still much higher in industrial regions like North America and the European Union than in developing nations.[21] A 2010 U.S. Geological Survey study of aluminum found that countries whose gross domestic product (GDP) per capita is less than $5,000 consume less than 5 kilos of aluminum per person; those whose GDP per person falls between $5,000 and $15,000 consume 5–10 kilos of aluminum per capita; but a per capita income of greater than $25,000 typically implies consumption of between 15 and 35 kilos.[22] Not surprisingly, wealthier countries have greater levels of aluminum in use—in buildings, vehicles, and myriad other economic outputs—than developing countries, often by a factor of three to ten.[23] If developing country prosperity implies similar levels of resource use, strong demand for resources will likely be the norm in the decades ahead.

High rates of one-time use of resources cannot continue indefinitely on a finite planet, yet growth rates of resource use have increased since 2000 compared to their already high levels in the twentieth century. Figure A-4 depicts the growth in extraction of eighty-six nonrenewable resources, including a surge in growth since 2001 (to the right of the vertical line), as materials extraction took off in step with economic growth in emerging economies in Asia and Latin America. Note, too, the minimal impact of the global recession of 2009: it slowed but did not reverse the use of non-renewables, and the pace quickly resumed once global economic output picked up.[24]

One result of the strong demand has been rising resource prices. U.S. Geological Survey (USGS) data for the eighty-six metals and minerals show that their prices, which on average fell by just under one percent per year between 1900 and 2000, turned upward sharply starting in 2002, increasing by 6.4 percent each year between 2002 and 2010. So great was the change of fortune that rising prices over the recent eight-year period fully offset the price declines of the entire twentieth century. Although some prices have softened recently because of a slowing Chinese economy, they have not returned to pre-2002 level, and the pressure on prices could well resume with renewed demand.[25]

In addition to the rising price of nonrenewables, a growing body of evidence suggests that market scarcity could become the norm for critical nonrenewable resources. Most critical is the fact that many resources, even if geologically plentiful, are increasingly energy-intensive to extract, making them difficult to get to market at affordable prices. For example, as

Figure A-4. World materials extraction, 1900-2011

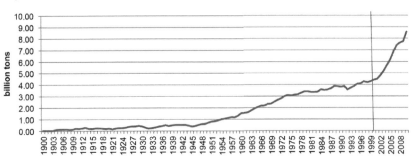

metal ore grades decline—meaning there is less and less recoverable metal in each rock—greater mining effort and more processing is required to extract a given quantity of metal. Average ore grade for copper, for example, has fallen from about four percent in 1900 to about 0.7 percent in 2012.[26]

Thus, two reinforcing trends are racing toward a collision that could translate to declining market availability of minerals in the near to medium term: energy scarcity could well limit minerals output even as declining concentrations and quality of minerals require ever-greater inputs of energy.

WHAT ABOUT RECYCLING?

Despite suggestions of scarcity, resources in most economies are still typically used only once, then tossed away. The United Nations' International Resource Panel determined in 2011 that for only eighteen of sixty metals is the recycled share of discarded metal—known as the end-of-life recycling rate—above fifty percent.[27] (See Table A-5.) High rates tend to apply to materials in easily recoverable applications, such as car manufacturing.[28] Lower rates are typical of small quantities of metal in complex products such as electronics.[29]

Table A-5. End-of-Life Recycling Rate for 60 metals

Recycling Rate	Number of metals	Metals
Greater than 50 percent	18	Aluminum, cobalt, chromium, copper, gold, iron, lead, manganese, niobium, nickel, palladium, platinum, rhenium, rhodium, silver, tin, titanium, zinc
25 to 50 percent	3	Magnesium, molybdenum, iridium
10 to 25 percent	3	Ruthenium, cadmium, tungsten
1 to 10 percent	2	Antimony, mercury
Less than 1 percent	33	Lithium, beryllium, boron, scandium, vanadium, gallium, germanium, arsenic, selenium, strontium, yttrium, zirconium, indium, tellurium, barium, hafnium, tantalum, thallium, bismuth, lanthanum, cerium, praseodium, neodium, samarium, europium, gadolinium, terbium, dysprosium, holmium, erbium, thulium, ytterbium, lutetium

Source: See endnote [30]

Indeed, many metal stocks end up in landfills. The U.S. Geological Survey observed in 2005 that the tonnage of aluminum in dumps in the United States was equal to about 43 percent of the aluminum in use in the U.S. economy.[31] For copper, stocks in dumps were about thirteen percent of stocks in use in the country, and for steel, the figure was twenty percent.[32] In fact, the USGS estimates that U.S. landfills hold enough steel to build 11,000 Golden Gate Bridges.[33]

For the United States, conservation of resources would seem to be prudent policy. Although the United States is often described as having an abundance of metal and mineral resources, it relies on imports to meet a great share of demand. Imports account for more than half of U.S. demand for forty-one of sixty-one metals and minerals whose trade is tracked by the United States Geological Survey. And for seventeen of those forty-one commodities, imports meet one hundred percent of demand.[34] Even rather plentiful resources may be of concern because of their importance. Phosphate rock, a key ingredient of fertilizer that has no known substitute and is therefore critical to agriculture, is relatively plentiful, but five nations account for ninety percent of global reserves, and one, Morocco, controls about seventy percent of the global total, raising concerns about food security. Thus, from many perspectives, conservation is of great strategic interest to the country.

In sum, the dual pressures of strong economic growth in the developing world, and increasingly difficult-to-access resources, sets up a conflict between resource demand and availability that could raise resource prices, dampen prosperity, and perhaps lead to political turbulence in societies worldwide. Unless greater effort is made to create circular economies that provide a high quality of life with a minimum of material input, consumption this century could have a very different and more difficult character.

POLLUTION

Modern economic activity generates pollution of all kinds, from air and water emissions to chemical releases, all of which harm human and non-human life alike. Most pollution impacts are felt at the local level, but some, like acid rain, are regional in scope, and still others, such as carbon pollution and ozone-depleting substances, are felt globally. Three sources of pollutants deserve special mention here.

Ground level ozone—Often described as "air pollution," ground level ozone is common in most cities of the world and severe in many. Ground level ozone levels in the Northern Hemisphere have doubled since the Industrial Revolution as a result of emissions of various gases from fossil fuel burning and agriculture—with powerful consequences. [35] Yields of staple crops, for example, are estimated to be as much as ten to twenty percent lower in industrial countries because of the pollution.[36] More important, the World Health Organization estimates that in 2012 about one in eight deaths globally was due to exposure to air pollution—in part because of indoor burning of biomass such as wood and cow dung for heating and cooking, but also because of outdoor air pollution.[37] And the number of deaths due to ground level ozone is expected to quadruple by 2030.[38]

Nitrogen—Although nitrogen makes up almost eighty percent of the atmosphere, it becomes damaging when it becomes reactive in the environment in amounts that cannot be absorbed by nature. The total amount of reactive nitrogen in the environment has increased with industrial activity, largely because of fossil fuel combustion and the production and use of nitrogenous fertilizers. Fossil fuels generate mono-nitrogen oxides (*nitric oxide* and *nitrogen dioxide* produced from the reaction of *nitrogen* and *oxygen* gases in the air during *combustion*), which pollutes the air, while fertilizers lead to eutrophication of waterways that produce "dead zones" in which no aquatic life can flourish. (See also the Oceans section.) Some ten cases of oxygen depletion were recorded in waterways worldwide in 1960, but there are five hundred today, and the number could increase as ocean temperatures rise with a warming climate.[39] Reactive nitrogen is expected to increase in quantity in step with food production and fossil fuel use. The challenge will be to ensure that less leakage of reactive nitrogen to the atmosphere and waterways occurs, even in the face of increased use.

Chemicals—Some 248,000 chemical substances are in use in the global economy today, and they seem to be found on every corner of the planet.[40] For example, more than ninety percent of water and fish samples from aquatic environments are contaminated by pesticides.[41] Although the impact on human health is not fully understood, the WHO reported that 4.9 million deaths were attributable to environmental exposure to chemicals in 2004.[42] Some effects are immediate and clear: some three percent of agricultural workers worldwide suffer an episode of chemical poisoning each year. Others develop over longer periods: persistent organic pollutants (POPs), a group of chemicals that persist in the environment and bioaccumulate, lead to disorders in neurological development, endocrine disruption, and cancer.[43] POPs have been found in regions as farflung as the Arctic and Antarctic. Meanwhile, new waste streams such as nanomaterials—whose basic building blocks are only one-billionth of a meter in size—are emerging, with very little understanding of their impact on human or environmental health.[44] Finally, the impact of chemicals is usually assessed on a substance-by-substance basis, with little understanding of how various chemicals interact with each other.[45]

FURTHER EXPLORATION

Ellen MacArthur Foundation at http://www.ellenmacarthurfoundation.org/
Tim Jackson, *Prospering Without Growth*
Annie Leonard, *The Story of Stuff*, at http://storyofstuff.org/
New Economics Foundation, at *http://www.neweconomics.org*

ECOLOGICAL FOOTPRINT

With contributions by Mathis Wackernagel, Ph.D.,
President of the Global Footprint Network

Human societies make large and growing demands on the goods and services our planet provides—from food, fish, and water to ecological services such as absorption of carbon dioxide. But how much demand is too much? The Ecological Footprint is an analytical tool that helps measure humanity's ongoing demand for the planet's ecological resources and services. It tracks people's demands for biologically productive areas of Earth's ecosystems, and compares this demand to the biologically productive areas available within a region or on the planet. Demand and biological capacity are both measured in "global hectares"—biologically productive hectares with world average productivity.

Global Footprint Network, an international sustainability think tank, maintains and updates the National Footprint Accounts calculations. These calculations assess the planet's biological capacity, or biocapacity, as the biologically productive area required to provide resources (such as agricultural area) and absorb waste like carbon dioxide (such as forested area). Global Footprint Network's latest published data shows global biocapacity to be twelve billion hectares.[46] This is the natural endowment available to support human and other forms of life on the planet. Meanwhile, humanity's Ecological Footprint is the biologically productive area needed to accommodate human demands for nature's goods and services. For 2008, this number was 18.2 billion hectares[47].

Thus, humanity's demands on the planet's biocapacity are about fifty percent greater than our planet can renew—in other words, it takes about one year and six months to regenerate what people demand from nature in one year. The only way to sustain this ecological overspending is by digging into nature's capital accounts. We catch more fish than the oceans can regenerate, for example, and we cut forests faster than they can grow back. Depleting stocks of fish, trees, and other resources, and accumulating waste such as carbon dioxide in the atmosphere and oceans is possible for a limited time, but it is not a lasting strategy: eventually fishing areas will be empty and forested area will be gone. Even if complete exhaustion of resources is decades away, the impacts of overexploitation are felt much sooner, often in the form of soaring prices for resources.

Global Footprint Network describes nations that use more ecological resources than their ecosystems can renew as "ecological debtors."[48] Whereas most societies through most of history were "ecological creditors," today eighty-five percent of the world population lives in countries that are ecological debtors. And the global population as a whole is running an ecological deficit.

Humanity's Ecological Footprint has fluctuated somewhat over time, while our planet's biocapacity has declined as ecosystems are degraded and lost. By the early 1970s, the global Ecological Footprint had surpassed the Earth's biocapacity, and the gap between the two—the ecological debt incurred by humanity—has grown larger since then.[49] We are in ecological overshoot. (See Figure A-6.)

Figure A-6. Global Ecological Footprint and Biocapacity

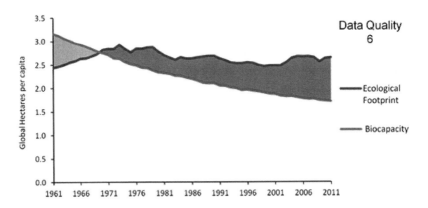

Not surprisingly, national Ecological Footprints come in a range of sizes. Wealthier countries tend to have larger footprints than developing countries. On a per capita basis, individuals in high-income countries have a greater footprint than people in low-income countries. Table A-7 shows the Ecological Footprint per person of various groups of countries, categorized by income, and the extent to which each group overshoots its biocapacity. [50]

At the national level, ecological debt also comes in various sizes. Table A-8 shows the top fifteen ecological debtors in the world, and reports their deficit as a share of biocapacity. Several countries with the highest levels of debt per unit of biocapacity are located in the Arab Gulf, where water scarcity is great and forest cover to absorb carbon emissions is lacking. But other countries, such as the United States, are in deficit largely because consumption levels are higher than their abundant resource endowment can support.

Some countries with ecological deficits import ecological goods and services to avoid drawing down their own natural capital. For example, a growing number of countries import "virtual" water, in the form of products and their processing. Countries that depend heavily on imports of virtual water include Jordan, Greece, Italy, Portugal, Spain, Algeria, Libya, Yemen, and Mexico.[51] But given that most countries are in ecological deficit, it is impossible for all countries to use a trade strategy that accommodates their overconsumption and addresses their national deficits.

Table A-7. Ecological Footprint per person of country groups by income level (2008)

Country Group	Biocapacity (global hectares per person)	Ecological Footprint (global hectares per person)	Overshoot (global hectares per person)
High Income	3.1	6.1	-3.0
Middle Income	1.7	2.0	-0.2
Low Income	1.1	1.2	-0.1
WORLD	1.8	2.7	-0.9

Table A-8. The world's 15 largest ecological debtors

	Ecological Footprint (global hectares per person)	Total Biocapacity (global hectares per person)	Ecological Deficit (global hectares per person)	Deficit as share of biocapacity (percent)
Singapore	5.3	0.0	(5.3)	30,000
Kuwait	6.3	0.4	(5.9)	1,500
Israel	4.8	0.3	(4.5)	1,400
South Korea	4.9	0.3	(4.5)	1,350
United Arab Emirates	10.7	0.8	(9.8)	1,200
Japan	4.7	0.6	(4.1)	700
Saudi Arabia	5.1	0.8	(4.3)	500
Netherlands	6.2	1.0	(5.2)	500
Belgium	8.0	1.3	(6.7)	500
Italy	5.0	1.1	(3.8)	340
Qatar	10.5	2.5	(8.0)	320
Switzerland	5.0	1.2	(3.8)	300
Macedonia TFYR	5.7	1.4	(4.2)	300
Spain	5.4	1.6	(3.8)	240
United States	8.0	3.9	(4.1)	110

FURTHER EXPLORATION

World Wildlife Fund, *Living Planet Report 2012* (Washington, DC: WWF, 2012)
Global Footprint Network, *Ecological Footprint Atlas* (Oakland, CA: GFN, 2010)
Global Footprint Network, "Why are Resource Limits Now Undermining Economic Performance?"

FOOD AND CROPLAND

Global food production today is cornucopian: more food, of greater diversity, is available to more people, in more places, than at any time in human history.[52] This soaring human achievement carries sobering caveats, however: some 795 million people—one out of nine of the human family—are undernourished, and hundreds of millions lack critical micronutrients such as Vitamin A and iron.[53] Moreover, progress in reducing hunger has been slow by any measure.[54]

More worrisome still, the steadily widening food security umbrella of the past century is hardly guaranteed to expand further in the decades ahead, because of two key pressures on the global agricultural system. On one hand, population growth, richer diets, and increased use of crops for fuel all drive up demand for agricultural products. At the same time, resource scarcity, especially of land and water, threatens the capacity of the world's farmers to meet the growing demand for food and fuel crops. In sum, while cheap, abundant food became the norm for a growing share of the human family over the twentieth century, this progress is by no means guaranteed to continue unless the dual challenges of steadily growing demand and constrained supply are reconciled.

GROWING DEMAND

A growing population places pressure on the world's farmers, as more food is needed to support healthy, dignified lives for all. Global population increased more than fourfold between 1900 and 2010, and is projected to expand by another thirty-six percent by 2050.[55] But other factors beyond raw increases in population also raise the demand for crops, including growing prosperity among the poor and demand for biofuels. All factors considered, the United Nations Food and Agriculture Organization (FAO) projects that global agricultural demand in 2050 will be sixty percent higher than in 2005/2007.[56]

Growing Prosperity—A poor person who sees an increase in income will typically add variety to his or her diet by supplementing grains and vegetables with sources of protein, typically from animals or fish, in the form of milk, cheese, meat, and eggs. The result can be a more interesting and healthful diet, but also an increase in the amount of grain required, as many livestock are grain-fed. Grain feeds many more people directly than when it is fed to cows, pigs, chickens, and fish to create meat for human consumption. So a person consuming livestock products is increasing pressure on the global food system to produce grains. This is happening today, millions of times over, as more poor people get a taste of prosperity in emerging economies worldwide and join wealthy consumers with long-established habits as meat eaters.

Demand for Biofuels—Production of biofuels (ethanol, biodiesel, and other fuels made from grains, sugar, and oilseeds) eat up nearly forty percent of coarse grain production in the U.S., fifty percent of Brazil's sugar crop, and eighty percent of oilseed production in the EU.[57] The United States Department of Agriculture projects that between 2013 and 2022 biodiesel production will grow by thirty percent, and ethanol by forty percent, in the seven countries that dominate the biofuel sector.[58] Demand for biofuels has contributed to rising food prices in the last decade: the FAO says that biofuels represent a "new market fundamental" that affects prices for all cereals.[59]

INTENSIFICATION: THE RESPONSE TO GROWING DEMAND

As demand for agricultural products grew by 2.2 percent per year between 1961 and 2007, the extent of arable land grew much more slowly—just fourteen percent for the entire period. [60] To meet demand, farmers intensified production, using mechanization, chemical fertilizer (in place of manure), new seed varieties, irrigation, and other advances to coax more output from each hectare of land. Meanwhile, as fish populations collapsed in many ocean areas, fishers also turned to intensification: aquaculture, or

Figure A-9. World Fish Production, Capture and Aquaculture, 1950-2013

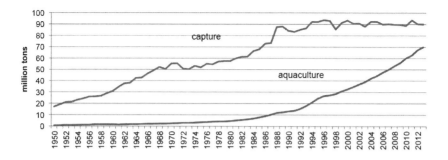

fish farming, became a key solution for meeting market demand for fish.[61] (See Figure A-9.) Farmers and fishers in the decades ahead will be challenged to continue to make each hectare and each fish farm yield ever greater quantities of food.

CONSTRAINED SUPPLY?

Whether humanity's success in increasing food production can continue under the pressure of growing demand is unclear. But the task will be made much harder as several trends combine to diminish the capacity and productivity of the agricultural system. Taken together, they suggest that adequate increases in agricultural productivity may be difficult to achieve at the global level and impossible to achieve in many countries.

Land Availability and Quality—Land suitable for farming, but not yet tapped, is not widely available in most of the world outside of Latin America and Africa. Indeed, the FAO reports that essentially zero additional suitable land remains in a belt around much of the middle of the planet, including countries in the Near East and North Africa, South Asia, and in Central America and the Caribbean.[62]

In addition, remaining land may be of low quality. Two studies since 1990 to assess degradation at the global level have suggested that some fifteen to twenty-four percent of the world's land is degraded.[63] The conclusions are approximations, as the science for such estimates is still imprecise. In addition, not all of the degraded land was agricultural land. Still, diminishment of double-digit shares of a foundational resource for food production is a serious concern. Moreover, the estimate in the second study—which measured degradation using a proxy yardstick, the decline in vegetative mass—has serious climate implications. Less vegetative mass means less atmospheric carbon is absorbed, leaving more carbon in the atmosphere to warm the planet.[64] Thus degraded land not only diminishes the productive capacity of farmland, but also weakens a key defense against climate change, which in turn further depresses food production overall, as discussed below.

Water Availability—Growing water stress is expected in the decades ahead: the United Nations projects that some 1.8 billion people will live in countries or regions with absolute water scarcity by 2025, while two-thirds of the world's people could live in conditions of water stress.[65] Water scarcity could impact one of the most productive pieces of agriculture, irrigated farmland, which accounts for forty-four percent of global crop production on only sixteen percent of arable land in use today.[66] Although irrigated area has expanded steadily for more than fifty years, area per person has steadily declined with population growth. (See Figure A-10.) Crucially, two regions with high rates of irrigation withdrawals (Near East/North Africa, and South Asia) are also regions the FAO identifies as having no new land to bring into cultivation. And they are areas of particular political volatility in recent decades.

Water scarcity will be exacerbated by climate change. A modeling effort published in 2013, which integrated the analysis of several climate models with that of models of agricultural output, found that climate change will raise the share of global population living under conditions of absolute water scarcity by forty percent, compared with the effect of population growth alone.[67]

Figure A-10. World Irrigated Area per Person

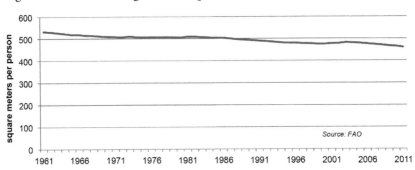

Fossil fuel dependence—Agriculture is an energy-intensive sector, accounting for about thirty percent of global energy consumption and producing more than twenty percent of global greenhouse gas emissions.[68] Tractors and trucks are powered by petroleum. Natural gas is critical to the manufacture of fertilizer and pesticides. Food processing, refrigeration, and packaging all require electricity, which is often supplied by fossil fuels. [69] Oil prices have remained at high levels for several years[70], and fossil energy increasingly requires more sophisticated technologies, at higher prices, to find and extract more remote resources, such as deepwater offshore deposits, or those that require greater processing, such as tar sands. Given agriculture's large appetite for energy, rising prices for fossil fuel will inevitably translate to higher food prices.

Climate change—Shifts in temperature and rainfall brought on by climate change will vary from region to region. But at the global level, a 2014 report by the Intergovernmental Panel on Climate Change (IPCC) noted that net production could decline by 0.2-2.0 percent per decade over the remainder of the century, even as demand increases by fourteen percent per decade.[71] Higher temperatures are projected to lower crop yields eventually and to increase the prevalence of weeds and pests. New rainfall patterns overall increase the risk of crop failures, and over the long run, of production declines.[72] The new patterns are expected to have much greater negative impacts in low-latitude (often developing) countries than in high-latitude (often wealthy) ones, and these divergent results are projected to widen over time.[73] The direct climate impacts on corn, soybeans, wheat, and rice—which provide the bulk of the human diet—have been projected to involve losses of eight to twenty-four percent of the calories produced today (and this assumes increased fertilization due to the increased carbon in the atmosphere). Add to these losses the climate-driven loss of irrigated area in the western United States, China, and West, South, and Central Asia, and production losses mount further. While climate change will also increase irrigated potential in some regions, including the northern and eastern United States, parts of South America, much of Europe, and Southeast Asia, substantial investments in irrigation infrastructure would be required.[74]

FOOD ENOUGH FOR ALL?

Even as demand for food continues to rise, national self-sufficiency in food is out of reach for a growing number of countries. Many nations choose to import food for economic or other reasons, but a growing number *must* do so because their capacity to raise crops lags behind the national demand for food. Various studies estimate that billions of people worldwide will live in countries that are not self-sufficient in food by 2050.[75] The shortfall in domestic production is especially acute in nations in the Middle East, North Africa, and the Andean region. For now, food trade picks up the slack in these regions and will grow in importance in the decades ahead, but whether all food needs can be met through trade is an open question.[76]

Even if trade can cover the gaps, having significant numbers of people dependent on other nations for their food raises a host of security, humanitarian, and governance challenges in the decades ahead.

FURTHER EXPLORATION

FAO, "The State of Food and Agriculture," 38th Session, Rome: FAO, 15-22 June 2013
  http://www.fao.org/docrep/meeting/028/mg413e.pdf
United Nations, World Water Development Report (annual series) (New York: United
  Nations, 2013)
Worldwatch Institute, Vital Signs Online, available at http://vitalsigns.worldwatch.org/
  trends/food-agriculture
Lester Brown, *Full Planet, Empty Plates: The New Geopolitics of Food Scarcity* (New York:
  W.W. Norton, 2012)

WATER

Earth is called the Blue Planet for its abundance of water, but much of our vast water endowment is unavailable for use by humans. Some 97.5 percent of water on our planet is seawater, while most of the 2.5 percent that is fresh water is locked in ice. Only 0.8 percent of all the water on Earth is freshwater available to humans and nature, either as surface water such as lakes and rivers, or as groundwater.[77]

Moreover, available water is not always located where it is needed. The United Nations notes that eighty-five percent of the world's people live in the driest half of the planet, for example.[78] And although water is a renewable resource that recycles regularly, its supply is fixed, so the continually growing global population means that water available per person will necessarily fall. Already, an estimated 783 million people lack adequate access to water, and nearly 2.5 billion people, about one out of three people on the planet, lack access to adequate sanitation.[79]

Table A-11. The Spread of Water Scarcity

Water Status	Number of Countries		Population
	1962	2011	2011
Water stressed	2	17	1.4 billion
Water scarcity	9	17	375 million
Absolute scarcity	12	29	458 million
Totals	23	63	2.27 billion

Source: See endnote[80]

A simple way to assess water scarcity is to review the water availability per person of a region. A country or region is said to experience "water stress" when annual water supplies drop below 1,700 cubic meters per person. Supply below 1,000 cubic meters per person renders an area "water scarce," while fewer than 500 cubic meters per person means that an area experiences "absolute scarcity." Using water availability per person, Table A-11, based on World Bank data, shows the growth in countries subject to

Table A-12. Countries classified as Water Scarce and Absolutely Water Scarce, 2011

Absolute Scarcity		Water Scarce	
Country	Fresh water per person (cubic meters)	Country	Fresh water per person (cubic meters)
Bahrain	3	Uzbekistan	557
United Arab Emirates	17	Antigua & Barbuda	590
Egypt	23	Hungary	602
Qatar	29	Somalia	606
The Bahamas	55	Cape Verde	612
Saudi Arabia	86	Sudan	641
Yemen	90	Netherlands	659
Maldives	90	Bangladesh	687
Israel	97	Cyprus	699
Mauritania	98	Burkina Faso	781
Jordan	110	Rwanda	852
Libya	115	Azerbaijan	885
Singapore	116	South Africa	886
Malta	121	Morocco	905
West Bank and Gaza	207	Zimbabwe	918
Niger	212		
Turkmenistan	275		
Moldova	281		
Barbados	284		
Algeria	298		
Pakistan	312		
Syrian Arab Republic	325		
Djibouti	354		
Tunisia	393		
St. Kitts and Nevis	453		
Oman	463		
Eritrea	472		
Kenya	493		

various levels of water availability per person, along with the 2011 population for each group. Already, nearly half a billion people live under very tight water supply conditions.

West Asia, North Africa, and Sub-Saharan Africa are among the countries experiencing the greatest levels of water scarcity. Table A-12 lists countries in 2011 that were absolutely water scarce and water scarce, based on internal renewable sources of freshwater.

Absolute scarcity does not necessarily translate to poverty or suffering: Singapore and Israel are both absolutely water scarce, yet they are far from impoverished. But avoiding human deprivation under such conditions requires water-centric policies and investments—and it leaves little room to absorb additional population growth or increases in water-intensive consumption. Indeed, as population expands in many water-tight countries, the number of people living under conditions of absolute water scarcity is set to skyrocket, from just under half a billion in 2011 to some 1.8 billion by 2025.[81]

Some countries import water-intensive products to reduce their own need for water. Jordan, for example, imports "virtual" water, in the form of products and their processing, that equals five times its own yearly renewable water resources. Other water-scarce countries that depend heavily on imports of virtual water (twenty-five to fifty percent) are Greece, Italy, Portugal, Spain, Algeria, Libya, Yemen, and Mexico.[82] In practice, such a strategy often translates to importing food, which saves huge quantities of water. But it also leaves many countries dependent on world markets for a growing share of their food supply.

GROUNDWATER

Groundwater is largely unseen, but it is a huge resource: its volume globally is about twenty-five times greater than the volume of all surface water (rivers, streams, lakes, and the like) on the planet.[83] Some 2.5 billion people depend solely on groundwater to meet their water needs,[84] and it is a critical input to some of the most productive agriculture in the world. But groundwater is increasingly overexploited in many subnational regions. A 2012 study in the journal *Nature* estimated that some twenty percent of the world's aquifers are being pumped faster than they can be recharged by rainfall. [85] It also found that almost a quarter of the world's population lives in regions where groundwater is being used up faster than it can be replenished. [86]

Satellites are increasingly used to document the depletion of aquifers. A 2002-2009 study revealed that the region encompassing the Tigris and Euphrates river basins had lost 144 cubic kilometers of fresh water, nearly equivalent to the volume of the Dead Sea, and that sixty percent of the loss was caused by overpumping aquifers. [87] The same satellite program documented a loss of 109 cubic kilometers' worth of water from Rajasthan, Punjab, and Haryana, key agricultural areas in India. [88] The depleted water is equal in volume to twice the capacity of India's largest reservoir. [89] Severe depletion is also documented by the satellite program in North China, North Africa, southern Europe, and the United States.

IMPACTS OF SCARCITY

Water is used extensively throughout any economy, affecting everything from manufacturing and energy production to health care and recreation. Here we briefly discuss the impact of water scarcity on agriculture, and the impact of climate change on water supply.

Agriculture—In most countries, no economic sector depends on water more than agriculture. Farming is the most water-intensive of all human activities, accounting for about two-thirds of water consumption at the global level. And for good reason: irrigation makes farming highly productive. While irrigated farmland accounts for only sixteen percent of arable land in use today, it accounts for forty-four percent of global crop production. [90]

Despite its vital importance, water is increasingly scarce in major agricultural regions. Some of the most-exploited aquifers in the world are in highly productive areas, such as the Central Valley of California and the High Plains of the United States, the North China Plain in China, the Nile Delta of Egypt, and the Upper Ganges of India and Pakistan. [91] On the North China Plain, which produces about half of all of China's wheat, groundwater is overpumped and wells are now dug more deeply, 120-200 meters compared with only twenty to thirty meters a decade ago. Pumping from such depths is energy-intensive and can be expensive, costing as much as half of a farmer's annual income. [92]

In addition, a growing number of river basins in agricultural areas are closed, meaning that water for domestic, agricultural, and industrial uses begins to compete with ecological needs. Agriculturally important river basins that are closed or nearly closed include the Amu and Syr Darya, the Indus, the Nile, the Colorado, the Lerma-Chapala, the Murray Darling, and Yellow River basins. The potential for expanded irrigation in these basins is quite limited.[93]

Agriculture's thirst for water will only grow with the growth in consumption of livestock products as developing countries prosper. A 2008 study found that the annual water requirement for food per person in China increased from 255 cubic meters per person in 1961 to 860 cubic meters in 2003, largely because of increased consumption of animal products.[94] Meanwhile, in industrial countries, a vegetarian diet is estimated to reduce water consumption by thirty-six percent.[95]

Climate change—Our warming planet throws a major disruptive wrench into the planet's water cycle by causing the cycle to *intensify* and *accelerate.*[96] Already, the following changes are under way:

- Average atmospheric water vapor content has increased since at least the 1980s
- Heavy precipitation events (those in which rainfall amounts are at or above the ninety-fifth percentile), have increased over large areas, especially at mid-latitudes
- Soil moisture, which is essential for crop growth, has decreased globally
- Droughts have become more intense and last longer
- Snow cover has decreased in most regions
- Freeze dates are later and thaw dates are earlier for river and lake ice in the northern hemisphere
- Glaciers and ice caps have lost considerable ice mass[97]

On balance, the negative impacts of climate change on water supplies are expected to outweigh the positive impacts, even though precipitation overall is expected to increase.[98] The IPCC has concluded that water stress and insecurity become more prevalent, not less, in a warmer and wetter world.[99] Indeed, the number of people living under absolute water scarcity is expected to increase by forty percent because of climate change, compared with the effect of population growth alone.[100]

FURTHER EXPLORATION

World Resources Institute, "Aqueduct Water Risk Atlas," at http://www.wri.org/resources/
maps/aqueduct-water-risk-atlas

"Water: A Special Issue," *National Geographic* magazine, April 2010, at http://ngm.national
geographic.com/2010/04/table-of-contents

"Worldwater" resource page of the Pacific Institute, at *http://pacinst.org/resources/*

BIODIVERSITY

By Brian Czech, Ph.D., President of the Center for the
Advancement of the Steady-State Economy

Biodiversity is the variety of life, from genes to ecosystems. Adequate biodiversity is essential to maintaining a hospitable environment for humans. A simple analogy is a house: diverse materials and designs are required to produce a fully functional dwelling that serves its occupants with security and comfort. Another analogy is clothing; a thread or two may be removed, but the loss of numerous threads will result in an unraveling that renders the garment useless. Earth's biodiversity is at great risk of unraveling in the twenty-first century, leaving humans with a highly inhospitable environment.

The most widely used measure of biodiversity is the species.[101] There are approximately 8.7 million species on Earth, including 7.8 million animal species, 300,000 plants, and 600,000 fungi.[102] Approximately 2.2 million of all species are marine. However, only about twenty percent of the species on

Table A-13. Numbers of known animal species

Species	Number	Share of all animal species (%)	Vertebrate Species	Number	Share of all vertebrate species (%)
Insects	963,000	73			
Arachnids	75,000	6	Fishes	24,900	48
Molluscs	70,000	5	Birds	9,880	19
Vertebrates	52,000	4	Reptiles	7,280	14
Crustaceans	40,000	3	Amphibians	5,200	10
Roundworms	25,000	3	Mammals	4,680	9
Other groups	99,000	6			

Earth have been documented. The approximately 1.75 million documented species are primarily animals and plants, with a much smaller number of other organisms.[103] Of the animal species on Earth, only about four percent are vertebrates (fishes, amphibians, reptiles, birds, and mammals, in order of their evolution) (See Table A-13).

EVOLUTION AND THE HISTORY OF BIODIVERSITY ON EARTH

Once life on Earth was firmly established approximately four billion years ago, biodiversity gradually increased and then proliferated as evolutionary pathways branched out in increasingly complex directions.[104] Eventually the growth rate of biodiversity slowed and biodiversity has waxed and waned since. Widespread and dramatic declines have occurred on numerous occasions, with five episodes of mass extinction documented.[105] Reasons for such declines included astronomical events, meteorological and geological events such as meteor impact, volcanism, and rapid climate change resulting from sudden atmospheric disturbance.

Major extinction episodes are extremely damaging to biodiversity. When many extinctions occur during a relatively short period of time, the effects reverberate throughout the ecosystem, causing widespread interference with evolutionary pathways and disrupting ecological processes. Not only are many species extinguished, but extinction prunes numerous limbs from the "tree of life," reshaping it forever.

The most dramatic decline in Earth's biodiversity was the Permian–Triassic extinction event, occurring at the end of the Permian period 252 million years ago. Approximately ninety-six percent of marine species and seventy percent of terrestrial species were extinguished.[106] Numerous causes have been hypothesized, including multiple meteor impacts, increased volcanism, and climate chnge.

BIODIVERSITY AND ECOLOGICAL INTEGRITY

Biodiversity is a primary element of ecological integrity or environmental health. However, maintaining ecological integrity is not synonymous with maximizing biodiversity.[107] Ecological integrity entails safeguarding or maintaining natural conditions, including the original or native species, genetic elements, ecosystems, and long-established ecological and evolutionary processes.[108]

Under natural conditions, biodiversity is typically high relative to the biodiversity occurring in highly modified landscapes. An extreme case of landscape modification is a densely developed urban core (for example, the Hong Kong financial district) in which most natural habitats and native species are absent. Under such conditions, biodiversity is very low, is highly unnatural, and may be typified by invasive and relatively undesirable elements such as rats, cockroaches, and pigeons.

Maintaining natural biodiversity is analogous to maintaining the numerous materials and structures of a well-functioning house. Allowing such biodiversity to erode puts the "occupants of the house" at great risk. To use an extreme but illustrative example, if the Earth's surface were one expansive financial district, it would be entirely unsustainable and unable to support the human population with all of its ecological, agricultural, extractive, and other needs. Long before such an untenable situation could arise, imbalance between humans and the rest of nature would threaten human existence.

SOME OF THE GOODS AND SERVICES PROVIDED BY BIODIVERSITY—AND AT STAKE TODAY[109]

Type	Examples
Provisional	Foods, fibers, timber, leathers, fuel wood, oils, pharmaceutical chemicals, ivory
Regulative	Climate regulation, erosion control, flood mitigation, population regulation (for example, of predators and prey) disease control, suppression of pathogens, water purification and regulation
Supportive	Primary production (photosynthesis), nutrient cycling and storage, pollination, soil formation, carbon sequestration
Cultural	Aesthetics, cultural heritage, sense of place, education, recreation, spirituality, religious meaning

Biodiversity worldwide is under severe threat by human population growth and economic activity. Cities and other human settlements have displaced wildlife habitats on a massive scale. Migration corridors and dispersal pathways have been eliminated or blocked.

The key principle is "competitive exclusion," whereby one species becomes more prominent by out-competing other species for resources.[110] Essentially, non-human life comprises the "economy of nature," and as the human economy grows, natural resources are inevitably re-allocated from the economy of nature to the human economy, where the resources are converted into manufactured capital, consumer goods, and waste.[111]

The re-allocation of natural resources from non-human species to the human economy has been a common theme of Earth's environment for approximately two million years.[112] However, this process accelerated dramatically during the Industrial Revolution with the development of petroleum-fueled technology and the discovery of vast stocks of fossil fuels.

Most species endangerment and extinction today stems directly from fossil-fueled economic activity (such as agriculture, logging, mining, commercial fishing, manufacturing, and the long list of services that proliferate in cities), along with economic infrastructure (power lines, canals, etc.), pollution, and the international trade and interstate commerce that introduces invasive species into new, vulnerable ecosystems. With the global human population and economy at all-time high levels of production and consumption, it is no surprise that ecologists speak of the current biodiversity decline as the "Sixth Great Extinction."

Rates of species endangerment and extinction are now orders of magnitude higher than background rates (that is, rates under typical ecological and evolutionary conditions). For example, since the passage of the Endangered Species Act in 1973, more than 1,519 species have been listed as threatened or endangered in the United States.[113] Only one of these species was considered endangered primarily by causes that are relatively unrelated to human economic activities.[114]

There is no single, consistent approach by which governments classify threatened and endangered species, so global estimates are difficult. However, a conservative estimate of imperiled plant and animal species would exceed 20,000.[115] It would also be rapidly growing and greatly supplemented by other types of species.[116]

A major development in our understanding of the conflict between economic growth and biodiversity conservation is the linkage of global warming to the growing, fossil-fueled economy.[117] Climate change is a severe threat to species and ecological integrity because temperature is one of the most influential variables in the life histories of species. A relatively sudden shift in average temperature (say, within a few decades) has dramatic ecological effects, and the whole complex of climate change (which also includes sea-level rise and changes in precipitation, soil moisture, fire behavior, regularly reoccurring biological events, and many other ecological variables) threatens the unraveling of ecosystems as we know them.

Some species have become icons of the threat of climate change and especially global warming: for example, polar bears, pikas, and even moose in some areas. The mammalian, high-latitude or high-altitude theme is no surprise, and global warming will push cold-weather species off the poles and mountaintops while relatively unprecedented evolutionary developments occur in tropical regions along the equator. It would be hard to conceive of an outcome that does not include proliferation of warm-weather and warm-water reptiles, amphibians, and fishes. Meanwhile, species ranges are shifting and ecosystems are being transformed throughout the planet.

Another aspect of climate change that threatens biodiversity is ocean acidification. As carbon dioxide increases in the atmosphere, approximately thirty to forty percent of it is dissolved into the oceans and other bodies of water. The result is a lowering of pH, and the rate of acidification is nearly unprecedented in Earth's geological history.[118] This is having substantial impacts on oceanic ecosystems, most notably coral reefs, which host some of the highest concentrations of biodiversity on Earth. Rates and levels of ocean acidification threaten to devastate marine life and ecosystems, which may not have the capacity to adapt to such abruptly changed conditions.

The geography of biodiversity erosion generally reflects biodiversity itself. All else being equal, areas rich in biodiversity are suffering the most rapid declines, at least in terms of absolute numbers of species. However, there is no region on Earth immune from rapid ecological transformation and biodiversity loss. Biodiversity loss and ecological transformation feed on each other: as biodiversity erodes, conditions for remaining species become less conducive to survival, and vice versa. The biodiversity crisis is clearly one of the most daunting and imminent threats to human wellbeing and even survival.

FURTHER EXPLORATION

American Museum of Natural History, Center for Biodiversity and Conservation, clearinghouse for biodiversity information, *http://www.amnh.org/our-research/center-for-biodiversity-conservation*

UN Convention on Biological Diversity, "Global Biodiversity Outlook 3," *http://www.cbd.int/gbo3/*

Peter Reich et al, "Impacts of Biodiversity Loss Escalate Through Time as Redundancy Fades," *Science*, Volume 336, Issue 6081, pp. 589-592.

World Health Organization, "Climate change and human health: Biodiversity" *http://www.who.int/globalchange/ecosystems/biodiversity/en/*

THE OCEANS

The world's oceans, which cover some three-quarters of the Earth's surface, are vital to creating sustainable economies worldwide—even for landlocked nations. Consider that oceans:

- *Provide food* to about a billion people who rely on fish, most of it marine-based, as their main source of animal proteins.
- *Generate economic activity*, through tourism, shipping, oil production, and fishing. The total economic value of oceanic goods and services is often estimated in the trillions of dollars.
- *Regulate the world's climate*, by circulating water and moderating temperatures.
- *Protect biodiversity*, including coral reefs, which are among the most species-rich ecosystems on the planet.
- *Provide vital services,* such as protection of coastal communities from storms provided by habitats like reefs, barrier islands, mangroves, and wetlands.[119]

Despite their importance, the world's oceans are overexploited and degraded at levels not seen in millions of years—to the point that these trends threaten massive changes to human societies.

GLOBAL FISH CATCH

Perhaps the best-known indicator of the decline in ocean health is the collapse of fisheries due to overfishing. Between 1950 and 1996, global marine fish catch increased more than fivefold, from fifteen million to eighty-four million tons.[120] But global catch has been flat since the early 1990s—nearly two decades' worth of annual output stuck at around eighty million tons—as fisheries have become increasingly depleted and as fishers have turned to lower quality stocks to make up for lost stocks. (See Figure A-14.)

Since 1950, fishing has become an industrialized endeavor dominated by technologies that enable intensive fishing practices—including drift nets, longlines, GPS, sonar, and onboard refrigeration. Fishing vessels became increasingly sophisticated, capable of capturing thousands of tons of fish, and of processing, packaging, and freezing them for quick sale once in port. The result has been progressive depletion of fisheries: The U.N.'s Food and Agriculture Organization reports that of fish stocks assessed as of 2009, eighty-seven percent are fully exploited or overexploited, meaning that the maximum sustainable production has been reached or exceeded.[122] (See Figure A-15.) Only 12.7 percent of global stocks were less

Figure A-14. Global Fish Catch, 1950-2012

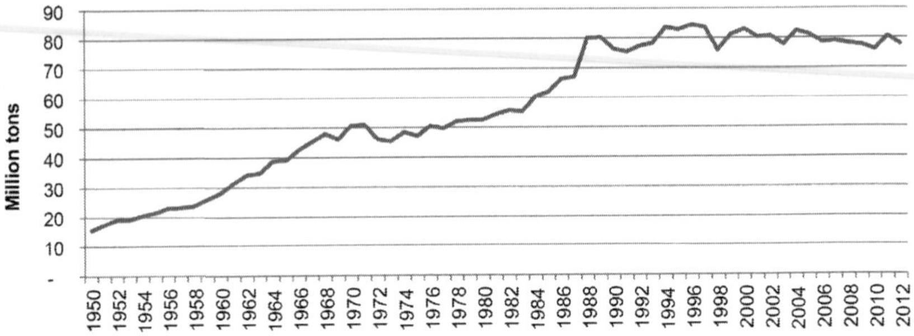

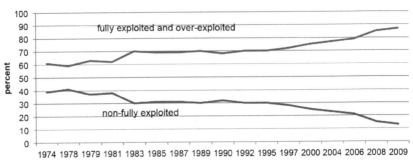

Source: See endnote [121].

Figure A-15. Trends in Marine Fish Stocks

Source: See endnote [125]

than fully exploited in 2009.[123] Other indicators of depletion paint an equally bleak picture. A 2005 study found that catch rates of large predatory fish—such as marlins, tuna, and billfish—have declined to about ten percent of their pre-industrial abundance. [124]

The plateauing of fish catch is not due to lack of fishing effort. A 2011 study found that various measures of effort, including total trawler engine power and number of fishing days per year, were roughly constant from 1950 to 1970, but have increased steadily since then—even after fish catch began to plateau in the mid-1990s. Similar to the extraction of oil, metals and many minerals, efforts to extract fish from the sea require ever-greater investment and energy just to keep output from falling.[126]

Although aquaculture has helped meet demand for fish as fish catch has stalled, it carries clear costs. Aquaculture replaces what had been freely provided good, wild fish, with farmed fish that must be fed, raised, and protected from disease.

OCEANIC DEGRADATION

While overfishing grabs the headlines, ocean pollution may be a far more troubling and long-term signal of declining ocean health. Pollution from carbon emissions and other human-generated activities is changing the basic chemistry of oceans worldwide and disrupting fish populations in hundreds of fisheries. Of particular concern are acidification, creation of "dead zones," and die-offs of coral reefs.

Acidification—The world's oceans are twenty-six percent more acidic than before the Industrial Revolution, the product of steadily rising levels of pollution.[127] Carbon emissions are a key concern: the oceans are a major depository of carbon, and about a quarter of humanity's annual atmospheric emissions of carbon end up there.[128] CO_2 reacts with seawater to lower the pH (raise the acidity) of the water. Today's acidification rate is estimated to be ten to one hundred times faster than at any time in the past fifty million years.[129] Acidification causes the shells and skeletons of "marine calcifiers"—corals, oysters, clams, mussels, and snails, in addition to phytoplankton and zooplankton that form the base of the marine food web[130]—to dissolve more readily as seawater becomes more corrosive from acidification. By the middle of the century oceanic accumulation of carbon dioxide is likely to be twice as great as prior to the industrial era, creating increased acidification pressures. Indeed, at continued high rates of carbon emissions, acidity could increase by 170 percent by 2100.[131]

Oceanic history provides clear warning signs of the harm from acidification. An increase in atmospheric carbon and oceanic acidification fifty-five million years ago—at rates far slower than today's—produced a mass extinction of some marine species, especially deep-sea shelled invertebrates.[132] Meanwhile, the Intergovernmental Panel on Climate Change observes that acidification of oceans over the rest of the century could produce ocean changes similar to those observed during the event fifty-five million years ago.

For all the trouble that ocean acidification portends, it is also credited with slowing the rate at which the planet is warming, because oceans have taken up carbon that would otherwise have remained in the atmosphere. But this blessing is likely to diminish: as the world's oceans warm and as oceans become saturated with carbon, the rate of accumulation is projected to fall. Some scientists argue that a slower rate of oceanic uptake of carbon is already underway.[133]

"Dead Zones"—As fertilizer runoff from farms flows into streams and rivers, then reaches the open sea, it creates nutrient-rich waters that fuel the growth of algae. The algae eventually die and sink to the sea bottom, where they are consumed by bacteria, a process that depletes the water of oxygen. Lack of oxygen drives away or kills fish and other marine life, resulting in a "dead zone" that can be quite sizable: the dead zone in the Gulf of Mexico, formed by runoff from farms in the midwestern U.S. that enters the Mississippi River and flows to the Gulf, was more than 15,000 square kilometers in 2013, about the size of Connecticut. With the intensification of agriculture since the 1960s and the consequent use of greater quantities of fertilizer, the number and extent of dead zones worldwide has spread dramatically. The United Nations Development Programme identifies more than 500 dead zones worldwide, affecting a total area of some 250,000 square kilometers, about the size of the United Kingdom.[134]

Coral Reef Decline—Another major sign of declining health of oceans is the state of coral reefs, among the most species-rich ecosystems on the planet. The National Oceanic and Atmospheric Administration reported in 2008 that the world had effectively lost nineteen percent of the original coral reef area, and that under business-as-usual assumptions (which ignore the impacts of climate change) another fifteen percent are seriously threatened with loss over the next decade or two.[135] As noted, acidification of oceans is a key source of coral decline, but warming seas and destructive fishing practices also take a toll.

The value of reefs to the environment and to humans is enormous. Although coral reefs cover less than one tenth of one percent of the ocean floor, they support some twenty-five percent of all marine fish species, making them a trove of biological wealth.[136] Reefs act as centers of spawning, refuge, and feeding for a wide range of species. And because reefs are rich in species, they are typically important fishing areas, especially in poor countries. In addition, reefs protect coastlines from storm surges and violent wave action, and are a growing source of ingredients for new medicines. The National Oceanic and Atmospheric Administration has estimated the value of reefs to be in the billions of dollars.[137]

FURTHER EXPLORATION

Daniel Pauly, "Aquacalypse Now," *The New Republic*, 28 September 2009

Food and Agriculture Organization of the United Nations, "Review of the state of world marine fishery resources," FAO Fisheries and Aquaculture Technical Paper 569 (Rome: FAO, 2011)

International Geosphere-Biosphere Programme, "Ocean Acidification: Summary for Policymakers," Third Symposium on the Ocean in a High CO_2 World (Stockholm: IGBP, 2013)

CLIMATE CHANGE

Climate change is arguably the most urgent issue on the entire sustainability agenda because of its global and disruptive impacts. The historic nature of the climate challenge, and the need to address it urgently, is captured in a 2014 article in the *New York Times* describing a draft report of the Intergovernmental Panel on Climate Change (IPCC), which is studying the impacts of climate change:

> *Nations have so dragged their feet in battling climate change that the situation has grown critical and the risk of severe economic disruption is rising, according to a draft United Nations report. Another 15 years of failure to limit carbon emissions could make the problem virtually impossible to solve with current technologies, experts found.*
>
> *A delay would most likely force future generations to develop the ability to suck greenhouse gases out of the atmosphere and store them underground to preserve the livability of the planet, the report found. But it is not clear whether such technologies will ever exist at the necessary scale, and even if they do, the approach would probably be wildly expensive compared with taking steps now to slow emissions.*[138]

Overcoming societal and individual lethargy regarding climate may be the greatest challenge of this and succeeding generations.

THE BACKSTORY

The basic science of climate change is straightforward. Various gases released through economic activities—most notably carbon, but also methane, nitrous oxide, and hyroflourocarbons and perfluorocarbons—

linger in the atmosphere, where they act like a blanket, trapping heat. The trapped heat makes the climate more volatile—storms are more frequent and intense, as are heat waves, cold spells, droughts, and floods. New temperature and precipitation patterns lead in turn to ecological changes that disrupt habitats, alter the relations among species, and throw a wrench into economic activity.

The IPCC has concluded that it is extremely likely that human influence has been the dominant cause of the observed warming since the mid-twentieth century. Here are highlights of the key scientific findings from its Fifth Assessment Report, completed in 2014:

- Earth's climate is warming, and many of the changes observed since the 1950s are unprecedented or unseen over millennia.[139]
- Each of the last three decades has been successively warmer at the Earth's surface than any preceding decade since 1850. In the Northern Hemisphere, 1983–2012 was likely the warmest thirty-year period of the last 1400 years.
- Over the last two decades, the Greenland and Antarctic ice sheets have lost mass, glaciers have shrunk almost worldwide, and Arctic sea ice and Northern Hemisphere spring snow cover have decreased in extent.
- The rate of sea level rise since the mid-nineteenth century has been larger than the mean rate during the previous two millennia.
- Concentrations of three key greenhouse gases (carbon dioxide, methane, and nitrous oxide) have increased to levels unseen in at least 800,000 years. Carbon dioxide concentrations have increased by forty percent since pre-industrial times.

The ocean has absorbed about thirty percent of the emitted anthropogenic carbon dioxide, causing oceans to become more acidic.

FUTURE IMPACTS

Climate change is projected to alter our planet's natural systems in numerous ways, with disruptive impacts for human societies.

More frequent and intense storms—Increased energy in the atmosphere from trapped heat intensifies water circulation from the land and oceans to the atmosphere and back, causing drought and floods to be more frequent and severe. Drought-prone land is vulnerable to flooding when rain does fall. In addition, hot temperatures and dry conditions increase the likelihood of forest fires. And the 2014 IPCC report notes that for every degree increase in temperature, an additional seven percent of the world's population will see a twenty percent decline in water resources.

Species migrations and extinctions—A warming world and new patterns of rain and snow are nudging trees, plants, and animals to move toward the poles and up mountain slopes. Some species such as polar bears may lose their habitat entirely. The IPCC estimates that twenty to thirty percent of species assessed are at growing risk of extinction from climate change impacts if global temperature increases exceed two to three degrees centigrade relative to its pre-industrial level.[140]

Sea level rise—Rising temperatures cause ocean water to expand and lead to rising seas. In addition, melting glaciers and ice caps add to sea level rise by adding more water to the oceans. Low-lying areas and islands are vulnerable to flooding. The IPCC report says sea levels are likely to rise by twenty-six to eighty-two centimeters by the end of the century, up from a range of eighteen to fifty-nine centimeters in its 2007 report,[141] which would affect cities such as Miami, New York, and Boston. But the largest human impact will be found in developing nations, where the IPCC estimates that hundreds of millions of people will be affected by coastal flooding and displaced due to land lost because of sea level rise.[142] Indeed, in some small island countries people have already had to abandon their land.

Health impacts—The risk of heat-related illness and death increases as temperatures rise. The World Health Organization (WHO) estimates that climate change may have caused more than 150,000 deaths in the year 2000 alone.

Economic Impacts—The 2014 IPCC report assessing climate impacts concluded that an average temperature increase of 2.5C above pre-industrial levels could produce economic losses of between 0.2 and 2.0 percent per year. This translates to a loss of more than a trillion dollars per year in 2012 (two percent of the 2012 global GDP of $71.8 trillion is $1.4 trillion), and more as the century unfolds. Climate change will reduce median crop yields by two percent per decade for the rest of the century, compared with an increase in demand of about fourteen percent per decade until 2050.[143]

Costs associated with climate change are not merely a future possibility, but are occurring today, and are substantial, according to a 2013 report from the Natural Resources Defense Council. It found that U.S. taxpayers paid nearly $100 billion in 2012—about $1,100 per taxpayer—to pay for damages from drought, storms, floods, and wildfires that year, all of which are exacerbated by climate change.[144] This is more than the federal government spends on education or transportation. What's more, taxpayers are shouldering more of the insurance burden for climate change, spending three times more than private insurers to pay for recovery from climate damages.[145]

Meanwhile, 2014 analysis by the risk assessment firm Maplecroft found that the sixty-seven countries it says face "high" or "extreme" risks from the impacts of climate change will account for nearly a third (thirty-one percent) of global economic output in 2025. Companies investing in developing nations to capture their middle-class market may find their investments to be highly at risk. The combined output of the sixty-seven is projected to be $44 trillion in 2025 and their combined population could top five billion.[146] The countries are assessed to be under threat from severe storms, flooding, drought, and other climate impacts. Maplecroft cites as an example Nigeria's loss of more than one-fifth of its oil output in the second half of 2012 because of extensive flooding. The ten most vulnerable countries, according to the Maplecroft analysis, are listed in Table A-16.

But other, larger economies, while not in the top ten, are also listed as "at extreme risk" because of climate impacts, including India (ranked twentieth), Pakistan (twenty-fourth) and Viet Nam (twenty-sixth). Economies in the high-risk category include Indonesia (thirty-eighth), Thailand (forty-fifth), Kenya (fifty-sixth), and China (sixty-first).

Climate change will reduce median crop yields by two percent per decade for the rest of the century, compared with an increase in demand of about fourteen percent per decade until 2050.

Table A-16. Nations Most Vulnerable to Impacts of Climate Change

Rank	Country
1	Bangladesh
2	Guinea-Bissau
3	Sierra Leone
4	Haiti
5	South Sudan
6	Nigeria
7	DR Congo
8	Cambodia
9	Philippines
10	Ethiopia

ACTION NEEDED

Some climate analysts support adoption of a global "carbon budget" of one trillion tons of carbon that can be burned if the global temperature increase is to be kept to under two degrees Celsius. Emissions of carbon since 1750 totaled 555 billion tons in 2011[147], so a trillion tons is just under double the amount already burned since the Industrial Revolution.[148] But while the first half trillion tons required more than 200 years to be burned, the next half trillion is projected to be burned in just twenty-five years or so, by around 2040.[149] Meeting this carbon budget will require discipline for two reasons: first, some three trillion tons of carbon are left in the ground in the form of fossil fuels, and continuing to rely heavily on fossil fuels is the path of greatest ease in the short run but great pain in the long term. Second, meeting the carbon budget will require huge investments and perhaps great sacrifice, an enormous political challenge when fossil fuels lie untapped in the ground.

FURTHER EXPLORATION

"Climate Progress," at http://thinkprogress.org/climate/issue/
"Real Climate," at http://www.realclimate.org/
United States Forest Service, "Climate Change Primer," at http://www.fs.fed.us/ccrc/climate
   -basics/climate-primer.shtml
"Accuweather Climate Blog" at http://www.accuweather.com/en/climate-change

OUR ECONOMIES

With contributions by Brian Czech, Ph.D.

Many of the problems described in Part Two are a function of modern, growing economies that depend on ever-greater resource use and ever-higher levels of consumption. In a "full-world economy," as award-winning ecological economist Herman Daly calls it, a new economic model is required that provides for the needs of all people while operating within limits set by nature. This new model is called the "steady state" economy: an economy that neither grows nor shrinks, but fluctuates mildly around a constant size.

Steady state economies were basically the norm for most of human history until the fossil-fueled Industrial Revolution. Additionally, the twentieth century was characterized by aggressive marketing and pro-growth policies and politics that promoted high levels of consumption. But for most of human history, while the global population slowly grew, the human population in any location would have seemed stable. This was also the case with per-capita consumption. Stable population and consumption are the primary ingredients of a steady state economy. The steady-state economy as proposed by Daly and elaborated on by scholars such as Brian Czech, Rob Dietz, and Dan O'Neill is meant to recover that macroeconomic stability, but at a higher plateau made possible by the advances in knowledge and capabilities since the Industrial Revolution.[150]

Steady state does not mean stagnant. Life can get continuously better in a steady-state economy, but what stabilizes is: 1) the use of natural resources and energy, sometimes called "throughput," and 2) population size. Economies would operate largely using materials already at hand and would be powered largely by renewable energy. People and societies would still *develop*; but production and consumption would not *grow*. A steady state economy can be seen as a major social development: not only would people's needs be met from a fixed resource base, but their vision of the purpose of life would shift from material consumption to pursuit of aesthetic achievements, community involvement, and other higher-level pursuits.

The Center for the Advancement of a Steady State Economy (CASSE) provides a useful summary (slightly modified below) of the misconceptions and truths behind a steady state economy:

Table A-17. Myths and Realities of a Steady State Economy

| Myth
A steady state economy...	Reality
..is another name for permanent depression, i.e., a failed growth economy.	A successful steady state economy is not a failed growth economy, but a different kind of economy. Just as a helicopter's core capacity is to hover rather than fly long distances, a steady state economy's core value is stability rather than growth. Stability in a steady state economy is a healthy condition that allows people to meet their needs without undermining the life-support systems of the planet.
...will cause technology and progress to grind to a halt.	A strong incentive for technological innovation exists in a steady state economy because of the drive for better and more sustainable goods and services.
...will lead to economic turmoil and mass unemployment.	This is true in a growth economy, where sluggish consumption produces recession. But a steady state economy is all about stability. Stability by definition eliminates turbulent boom and bust cycles and provides a good life for citizens.
... means widespread poverty.	A stable and sustainable population in a steady state economy will allow more resources per person than a growing population. Couple this with a fair distribution of wealth, and poverty becomes a thing of the past.
... is unnecessary because the economy can grow continually by decoupling growth from resource use and waste production.	We need to stabilize resource use in total, not just use resources more efficiently. Efficiency gains only prolong the limits to growth. Consider the fact that Americans use energy and water more efficiently today than forty years ago, but total consumption has increased dramatically.

Myth A steady state economy...	Reality
...is unnecessary because technological progress will stoke unlimited economic growth.	The laws of thermodynamics establish that, regardless of technology, all production requires resources and generates wastes. In addition, the second law of thermodynamics establishes that we cannot achieve 100% efficiency in the production process. When the limits to efficiency have been reached, the only way to grow the economy is by using more natural capital (including energy), which is limited in quantity.
... means government by a harsh communist regime.	A steady state economy can exist in a democracy with a common-sense mixture of markets and market regulations. Market structures are employed to allocate resources efficiently, but some vital decisions (e.g., how big to grow) are managed with fiscal and monetary policy. A steady state economy features a mix of private and public ownership of economic resources, just as the American economy always has.

GETTING TO A STEADY STATE ECONOMY

Efforts to create a steady state economy, especially of a size that is similar to the current economy, will require a somewhat different mindset about production and consumption. For example, if energy sources are to become increasingly renewable, a shift away from fossil fuels will be needed. And if raw materials are to be used at a sustainable rate, a comprehensive societal effort to conserve remaining stocks and to reuse materials already in the economy will be needed. The challenge is to increase resource productivity markedly, just as labor productivity increased greatly in the twentieth century. This is likely achievable: analysts have long asserted that fivefold increases in material productivity are possible in industrial economies.[151]

One conceptual framework for large and steady increases in resource productivity, known as a "circular economy," emphasizes meeting economic needs using a minimum of natural resources. By eliminating the wasteful one-way flow of resources that characterizes industrial economies today, a circular economy reduces the need for additional natural resources and the environmental degradation associated with extractive activities. Creating a circular economy requires policies designed to conserve natural resources, especially nonrenewables, as well as policies that generate more prudent patterns of production and consumption.

A circular, steady state economy features policies that treat nonrenewable resources as what they are: scarce and finite assets. Elimination of public subsidies for the extraction and use of nonrenewable minerals and fuels may be a logical place to start. For example, nonrenewable resources may be taxed at their source—at the mine shaft and the oil well—to encourage conservation. Many countries already tax mining—but not at levels that discourage the further extraction of nonrenewables and encourage the development of recycling programs and product remanufacturing. Incentives for recycling would help create employment (recycling is more labor-intensive than mining, for example) and would conserve resources.[152]

Governments can help create an ethic of resource conservation throughout their economies. In 2011 the European Commission released a *Roadmap to a Resource Efficient Europe* with the goal of making waste an essentially obsolete concept by 2020, with discarded material fed back into the economy as raw materials. This ambitious goal is severely challenged by the second laws of thermodynamics, which establishes that the utility of any given throughput invariably declines—heat dissipates and materials erode—but certainly a major reduction in waste flow is entirely possible. "Take-back" laws require producers to re-assume responsibility for products at the end of their useful lives, creating a strong incentive for companies to reduce the materials used in products and packaging and to make them recyclable or re-manufacturable. San Francisco is well on its way to its goal of "zero waste to landfills," with some eighty percent of waste composted or recycled in 2012. Such policies save energy and materials: studies at the Massachusetts Institute of Technology and in Germany have found that some eighty-five percent of the energy and materials embodied in a product are preserved in remanufacturing.[153]

Of course, achieving such gains economy-wide requires changes in how goods are produced. Products must be designed for recycling, like the parts on BMW automobiles that are bar-coded with information about metal content and recycling possibilities. Finally, technologies for materials separation and recycling must be improved to make recycling more economical.[154]

On the consumption side, a steady state economy entails meeting demand in creative ways that reduce throughput. Table A-18 summarizes many of the initiatives now underway to reduce the material and energy

Table A-18. Innovative Practices That Reduce Consumption of Materials and Energy

Innovation	Description	Example
Eco-industrial parks	Discards from one production process become inputs to another	China is particularly ambitious, having created more than 50 eco-industrial parks. In Guigang City, wastes from a sugar refinery, paper plant, cement mill, thermo-electric plant, and local farms are used as inputs to others' operations.
Whole system design	One process serves multiple purposes	Cogeneration uses the waste heat from electricity generation to heat and cool buildings and to heat water, achieving energy efficiencies of 65–75 percent compared with 45 percent when electricity generation and heating/cooling are provided separately.
Intelligent design	Advantages are sought wherever possible	Bus rapid transit (BRT) systems, conceived in Brazil, offer the high-speed advantages of a subway system at the lower cost of surface transportation. Passengers prepay and can board quickly, and buses have dedicated lanes and driver control of stoplights. By making public transport more attractive and affordable, BRT reduces the demand for material-intensive private cars.
Shared use	Goods serve multiple users	Dozens of tool libraries, toy libraries, and other sharing institutions give people access to infrequently used goods. Portland, Oregon, has three tool libraries, for example. A survey of more than 6,000 car-sharing participants in North America found that cars per household fell from 0.47 to 0.24 after signing up for carsharing.
Competitive efficiency	Efficiency improvements are benchmarked and ratcheted upward	A Japanese government program designates the most energy-efficient consumer products as "Top Runners" and challenges all products to meet the Top Runner standard within five years. Goals for 21 major energy-using consumer products have been met—and often exceeded.

requirements for meeting human needs.[155] In addition, governments can combat consumerism and steer consumption in resource-lite directions by taxing consumption rather than income (with a design that protects consumption of basics such as food and shelter), subsidizing solar panels and other technologies that shift consumption away from nonrenewables, and using government procurement power to expand the market for goods with high-recycled content or with other sustainability advantages.

Finally, a steady state economy requires a consumption ethic very different from the "shop 'til you drop" philosophy common in consumer-driven economies today.[156] In place of a strong consumerist orientation, citizens would find more happiness and greater purpose in personal relationships, community involvement, and enjoyment of resource-lite activities such as arts and sports and continuing education. They would seek goods designed to last, perhaps following the ancient native wisdom of thinking seven generations into the future. They would be motivated not to increase their material holdings, but instead to strive for personal and societal advance and development—learning to speak another language and playing an instrument, for example, or joining in a community effort to build a park or create a neighborhood band. The goal is a higher quality life rather than a higher level of consumption.

FURTHER EXPLORATION

Center for the Advancement of a Steady State Economy (CASSE) at www. http://steady state.org/

Batker, David and John de Graaf, *What's the Economy for, Anyway? Why It's Time to Stop Chasing Growth and Start Pursuing Happiness* (New York: Bloomsbury Press, 2011)

Berry, Wendell, *What Matters? Economics for a Renewed Commonwealth* (Berkeley: Counterpoint Publishers, 2010)

Czech, Brian, *Supply Shock: Economic Growth at the Crossroads and the Steady State Solution* (Gabriola Island, Canada: New Society, 2013)

Daly, Herman, *Beyond Growth: The Economics of Sustainable Development* (Boston: Beacon Press, 1997)

TO RECAP THE MESSAGE OF THIS BOOK, WE NEED TO:

- Recognize that we are now on a path leading to catastrophe.
- Understand and accept what we really are. Recognize that our minds evolved to live sustainably as hunter-gatherers but not in the world we now have.
- Become more than what we are.
- See the world as a unified whole and interact with it as such, holistically.
- Find more effective ways to reach others and convince them of our predicament.
- Work together. By working together environmentalists and environmental organizations can develop new techniques to move beyond our current stalemate and make real progress toward sustainability.

Please, if you have suggestions or ideas of what concerned individuals and organizations can do to increase our effectiveness and help us get on a path toward sustainability, pass them on to those who can use them, and to me (pseidel@fuse.net). I will collect them and make them available wherever and to whomever I can. Also visit my website at peterseidelbooks.com.

ABOUT PETER SEIDEL

 After having been a farmhand, factory worker, Alaska salmon fisherman, and carpenter, Seidel became a student of architect Mies van der Rohe and city planner Ludwig Hilberseimer. Around 1960, while working in Chicago on office and institutional buildings that he came to realize were environmentally damaging, he read a book describing the dangers of excessive population growth and looming resource shortages. Disturbed by this, he turned to teaching (over time, at five different institutions including universities in China and India) and developing ideas on environmentally and socially sustainable communities. This led to employment as master planner for a community of 60,000 outside of Cincinnati, Ohio. When this project was halted because of funding problems, he took up developing, designing, and building energy-conserving urban infill projects on vacant inner-city parcels.

As public interest in sustainability evaporated after the end of the Arab oil boycott during the Reagan Administration, Peter started to investigate the troublesome question of why, when we understand the many environmental dangers we face, we don't take meaningful action to deal with them. This led to publishing a number of articles in academic journals on this subject and three books: *Invisible Walls: Why We Ignore the Damage We Inflict on the Planet...and Ourselves*, Prometheus Books, 1998; *Global Survival: The Challenge and Its Implications for Thinking and Acting*, edited by Ervin Laszlo and Peter Seidel, SelectBooks, 2010; and a novel dramatizing the likely future consequences of environmental neglect and indifference, *2045: A Story of Our Future*, Prometheus Books, 2009. Website, http://www.peterseidelbooks.com/

175

ABOUT GARY GARDNER

 Gary Gardner is a Senior Fellow at the Worldwatch In-
stitute, an environmental research organization based
in Washington, D.C. He has written on a broad range of
sustainability issues, from cropland loss and water scarcity to malnutrition and bicycle use. Gary contributes
regularly to Institute publications, including *State of the
World and Vital Signs*. He is the author of the 2006 book
Inspiring Progress: Religions' Contributions to Sustainable Development. In
addition to his research and writing, Gary has done interviews in both English and Spanish with international media outlets including the BBC, Voice
of America, National Public Radio, and the *Los Angeles Times*.

Before joining Worldwatch in 1994, Gary was project manager of the
Soviet Nonproliferation Project, a research and training program run by
the Monterey Institute of International Studies in California. There, he
authored *Nuclear Nonproliferation: A Primer*, which is also published in
Spanish and Russian. He has also developed training materials for the
World Bank and for the Millennium Institute in Arlington, Virginia.

Gary holds master's degrees in Politics from Brandeis University and in
Public Administration from the Monterey Institute of International Studies.
He earned his bachelor's degree from Santa Clara University in California.

ACKNOWLEDGMENTS

In addition to those noted in the Preface, I am also grateful to a select group of individuals I gave the manuscript to and asked for comments: Regina Moulton, Jon Moulton, Arlen Westbrook, Mary Argus, Clayton Collier-Cartaino, Dave Simcox, Bruce Murray, John Bossert, Dick Bozian, Ralph Cautley, Bernadene Zennie, Gregg Hass, Dorothy Glanzer, Mary Anne Curtiss, and anyone I may have inadvertently left out.

Locating the owners of suitable graphics was a time-consuming and difficult job. I want to thank MaryLauren Malone for spending many hours helping me with that, because it would have been more than I could have handled alone. Robert Engelman has my gratitude as well, for connecting me to Gary Gardner, senior researcher at the Worldwatch Institute, who coordinated and wrote most of Part Two. Thanks too, to Brian Czech, Ph.D., who wrote one section of same and contributed to another, and Mathis Wackernagel, Ph.D., who provided material on our global footprint.

Many thanks as well to Christine Brooks and George Lois, who worked their magic to make this a handsome and professional-looking volume.

I am especially grateful to my outstanding editor, Carol Cartaino, without whom this book could not have gotten off the ground. Her editing and ideas and other help have left their mark throughout these pages.

ENDNOTES

PART ONE

1   Wilson, Edward O., *The Social Conquest of Earth* (New York: Liveright Publishing, a division of W.W. Norton, 2012), p. 7.

2   Most of these numbers from, or derived from: Brown, Lester R., *Full Planet, Empty Plates* (New York: W.W. Norton and Company, 2012).

3   http://www.footprintnetwork.org/en/index.php/GFN/page/world_footprint/

4   James, William, (1910), "The Moral Equivalent of War," *Popular Science Monthly*, 77: 400–410.

5   http://www.spiegel.de/international/world/0,1518,709135,00.html

6   Diamond, Jared, *The World Until Yesterday: What Can We Learn from Traditional Societies?* (New York: Viking Press, 2012), p. 358.

7   Pinker, Steven, *"The Better Angels of Our Nature: Why Violence Has Declined* (New York: The Penguin Group, 2011).

8   Lovett, Richard A., "What If the Biggest Solar Storm on Record Happened Today?," *National Geographic News*, March 2, 2011, and see Kappenman, John, "Geomagnetic Storms and Their Impacts on the U.S. Power Grid," Metatech Corporation, prepared for Oak Ridge National Laboratory, Meta-R-319, January 2010, pp. 2-29.

9   Hansen, James, *Storms of My Grandchildren* (New York: Bloomsbury Press, 2009), p. 236.

10 Jose Ortega y Gasset, *The Revolt of The Masses,* (New York: W.W. Norton 1930, 1932, & 1957;), p. 90.

11 Wilson, Edward O., *The Social Conquest of Earth* (New York: Liveright Publishing, division of W.W. Norton, 2012), p. 7.

12 Wilson, Edward O., *The Future of Life* (New York: Alfred A. Knopf, 2002), p. 40.

13 David Anderson, Charlie Rose brain series, PBS, October 5, 2010, episode eight

14 Storr, Anthony, *Human Destructiveness* (London: Grove Weidenfeld, 1991; New York: Ballantine Books, 1992), p. 21.

15 Storr, Anthony, *Human Destructiveness*, p. 15.

16 Le Bon, Gustave, *The Crowd* (New York: Viking Press, 1960), p. 26.

17   Haney, Craig, Banks, Curtis, & Zimbardo, Philip, "Interpersonal Dynamics in a Simulated Prison," *International Journal of Criminology and Psychology*, Vol. VI., 1968, pp. 279-80.

18   Kristof, Nicholas D. and WuDunn, Sheryl, *China Wakes* (New York: Random House, 1994), p. 73.

19   http://philanthropy.com/article/America-s-Generosity-Divide/133775/ The Chronicle of Philanthropy website, Aug. 20, 2012.

20   Anwar, Yasmin, "Media Relations," *UC Berkeley News*, February 27, 2012.

21   Teresa, Vincent with Renner, Thomas C., *My Life in the Mafia* (Greenwich, Conn.: Fawcett Publications, 1974, after Doubleday and Co., Inc., 1973), pp. 108 & 145.

22   Campbell, Jeremy, *The Improbable Machine: What the Upheavals in Artificial Intelligence Research Reveal About How the Mind Really Works* (New York: Simon & Schuster, 1989), p. 233.

23   http://www.epa.gov/climatechange/science/causes.html

24   Festinger, Leon, *When Prophecy Fails* (New York, Harper & Row, 1964), p. 3.

25   Storr, Anthony, *Human Destructiveness*, p. 142.

26   Storr, Anthony, *Human Destructiveness*, p. 124.

27   Browning, Christopher R., *Ordinary Men* (New York: HarperCollins Aaron Asher Books, 1992).

28   David Anderson, Charlie Rose brain series, PBS, October 5, 2010, episode eight.

29   Dana, Nuccitelli, posted by *The Guardian*, 16 May 2013.

30   http://www.gallup.com/poll/161645/americans-concerns-global-warming-rise.aspx

31   The Environmental Pollution Panel of the President's Science Advisory Committee, *Restoring the Quality of Our Environment* (Nov. 1965), The White House, Washington, D.C., pp. 111-133.

32   Vogt, William *Road to Survival* (New York: William Sloan Associates, 1948). Quote appears on dust jacket of original edition.

33   Lieberman, Danielle E., *The Story of The Human Body: Evolution, Health, and Disease* (New York: Pantheon Books, 2013), p. 13.

34   Stout, Martha, *The Sociopath Next Door*, (New York, Broadway Books, 2005), p. 8.

35   Richard Dawkins, *The Selfish Gene* (Oxford and New York: Oxford University Press, 1989).

36   Quoted from a U.S. National Park Service exhibit in Seward, Alaska.

37   Lowen, Walter with Mike, Lawrence, *Personality Types: Systems Science Explanation* (North Charleston, SC: BookSurge Publishing, 2006).

38   Kahn, Alan R., *Mind Shapes* (St. Paul, MN: Paragon House, 2005).

39   Simon, Herbert A., *Administrative Behavior, Third Edition* (New York: The Free Press, 1976), pp. xxix & xxx.

40   Asahi Glass Foundation, Tokyo, Japan, Results of the 21st Annual Questionnaire on Environmental Problems and the Survival of Humankind, Nov. 2012, p. 82.

41   Boulding, Kenneth, *Evolutionary Economics* (Beverly Hills, CA: Sage Publications, Inc., 1981), p. 173.

42 Gibb, C. A., "Leadership," in G. Lindzey & E. Aronson, eds., *Handbook of Social Psychology, Volume 4, Second Edition* (Reading, MA: Addison-Wesley, 1969), p. 218.

43 Ortega y Gasset, José, *La rebelión de las masas [The Revolt of the Masses]*. Published in Spain in 1930, and in the U.S. in 1932 and 1957 by W.W. Norton, pp. 14-15.

44 Ibid, p.18.

45 "A Cult of Ignorance," *Newsweek*, 21 January 1980.

46 Senator Al Gore, *Earth in the Balance* (New York: Houghton Mifflin, 1992), p. 305.

47 Herz, John H., *The Nation-State and the Crisis of World Politics* (New York: David McKay Co., 1976), pp. 9-10.

48 http://topforeignstocks.com/2010/09/06/duration-of-stock-holding-period-continues-to-fall-globally/

49 Fromm, Erich, *Escape From Freedom,* (New York: Holt, Reinhart, and Winston, Avon Books, 1965), p. 150.

50 Cohen & Solomon, " 'Crime Times' News Exploits Fears," *Liberal Opinion Week* (Creators Syndicate, Inc., June 27, 1994).

51 Seidel, Peter, "Is It Inevitable That Evolution Self-Destruct?" *Futures*, Elsevier, Amsterdam, Vol. 41, No. 10, Dec. 2009, pp. 754-9.

52 Seidel, Peter, "To Achieve Sustainability," *World Futures: The Journal of General Evolution*, Taylor and Francis, London, Vol. 67, No. 1, 2011, pp. 11-29.

53 Gazzaniga, Michael S., *Nature's Mind* (New York: Basic Books, 1994), p. 137.

54 Myers, David G., "The Social Psychology of Stability," *Global Survival*, eds. Ervin Laszlo and Peter Seidel (New York: SelectBooks, 2006), pp. 101-113.

55 Federal Reserve Bank of St. Louis, https://www.stlouisfed.org/publications/re/articles/?id=1860.

56 http://hub.aa.com/en/aw/power-of-storytelling?zonemode=page_2

57 Erik Assadourian and the Worldwatch Institute, *State of the World 2013: Is Sustainability Still Possible?* (Washington, D.C.: Island Press, 2013), pp. 113-125.

PART TWO

1 Worldwatch calculation based on: 1900 population is an average of values cited at United States Census Bureau, "Historical Estimates of World Population," at https://www.census.gov/population/international/data/worldpop/table_history.php; 2010 estimate from United Nations, Department of Economic and Social Affairs, Population Division, Population Estimates and Projections Section, online database, at *http://esa.un.org/unpd/wpp/unpp/panel_population.htm*; 2050 estimate from United Nations, op. cit. this note.

2 Department of Economic and Social Affairs, "World Population Prospects, the 2012 Revision" (New York: United Nations, June 2013) at http://esa.un.org/wpp/

3 Department of Economic and Social Affairs, "World Population Prospects the 2012 Revision" (New York: United Nations, June 2013) at http://esa.un.org/wpp/

4   United Nations, *The Millennium Development Goals Report 2013* (New York: United Nations, 2013) at http://www.un.org/millenniumgoals/pdf/report-2013/mdg-report-2013-english.pdf

5   United Nations, *The Millennium Development Goals Report 2013* (New York: United Nations, 2013) at http://www.un.org/millenniumgoals/pdf/report-2013/mdg-report-2013-english.pdf

6   United Nations, *The Millennium Development Goals Report 2013* (New York: United Nations, 2013) at http://www.un.org/millenniumgoals/pdf/report-2013/mdg-report-2013-english.pdf

7   United Nations, *The Millennium Development Goals Report 2013* (New York: United Nations, 2013) at http://www.un.org/millenniumgoals/pdf/report-2013/mdg-report-2013-english.pdf

8   Credit Suisse Research Institute, "World Wealth Report 2013" (Zurich: Credit Suisse AG, October 2013), p. 22 at https://publications.credit-suisse.com/tasks/render/file/?fileID=BCDB1364-A105-0560-1332EC9100FF5C83

9   Ricardo Fuentes-Nieva and Nick Galasso, "Working for the Few: Political Capture and Economic Inequality" (Oxford, UK: Oxfam International, January 2014) at http://www.oxfam.org/sites/www.oxfam.org/files/bp-working-for-few-political-capture-economic-inequality-200114-en.pdf.

10   Ricardo Fuentes-Nieva and Nick Galasso, "Working for the Few: Political Capture and Economic Inequality" (Oxford, UK: Oxfam International, January 2014) at http://www.oxfam.org/sites/www.oxfam.org/files/bp-working-for-few-political-capture-economic-inequality-200114-en.pdf

11   Credit Suisse Research Institute, "World Wealth Report 2013" (Zurich: Credit Suisse AG, October 2013), p. 22 at https://publications.credit-suisse.com/tasks/render/file/?fileID=BCDB1364-A105-0560-1332EC9100FF5C83

12   Department of Economic and Social Affairs, United Nations, "International Decade for Water for Life," webpage at http://www.un.org/waterforlifedecade/scarcity.shtml

13   Malin Falkenmark, "Growing water scarcity in agriculture: future challenge to global water security," Phil Trans R Soc A at http://www.water.ox.ac.uk/wordpress/wp-content/uploads/2013/10/Phil.-Trans.-R.-Soc.-A-2013-Falkenmark-.pdf

14   Nikos Alexandratos and Jelle Bruinsma, "World Agriculture Towards 2030/2050: The 2012 Revision" (Rome: FAO, June 2012) at http://www.fao.org/docrep/016/ap106e/ap106e.pdf, pp. 61 and 95.

15   International Union for the Conservation of Nature (IUCN), "Table 1: Number of threatened species by major groups of organisms," from the IUCN Red List, at http://cmsdocs.s3.amazonaws.com/summarystats/2013_2_RL_Stats_Table1.pdf

16   H. Stuart, et al., "Global Biodiversity: Indicators of Recent Declines," *Science* 28 May 2010, at http://www.sciencemag.org/content/328/5982/1164.full.html

17   World Business Council for Sustainable Development, "Sustainable Consumption Facts and Trends," http://www.fusbp.com/pdf/WBCSDSustainableConsumption.pdf

18   Yuval Atsom et al, "Winning the $30 Trillion Decathlon: Going for Gold in Emerging Markets," *McKinsey Quarterly*, August 2012, p. 4.

19   World Business Council for Sustainable Development, "Sustainable Consumption Facts and Trends," http://www.fusbp.com/pdf/WBCSDSustainableConsumption.pdf

20   World Business Council for Sustainable Development, "Sustainable Consumption Facts and Trends," http://www.fusbp.com/pdf/WBCSDSustainableConsumption.pdf

21   World Steel Association, *Steel Statistical Yearbooks* (Brussels: various years).

22   W. D. Menzie et al., *The Global Flow of Aluminum from 2006 through 2025* (Reston, VA: USGS, 2010).

23   T. E. Graedel, *Metal Stocks in Society: A Scientific Synthesis* (Paris: International Resource Panel, United Nations Environment Programme (UNEP), 2010).

24   Figure X from Thomas D. Kelly and Grecia R. Matos, "Historical Statistics for Mineral and Material Commodities in the United States," web database at http://minerals.usgs.gov/ds/2005/140/; Figure encompasses data for eighty-five metals and other nonrenewable materials.

25   Worldwatch calculation based on data in Thomas D. Kelly and Grecia Matos, *Historical Statistics for Mineral and Material Commodities in the United States*, Data Series 140 (Reston, VA: USGS, 2011); Richard Dobbs, Jeremy Oppenheim, and Fraser Thompson, "Mobilizing for a Resource Revolution," *McKinsey Quarterly*, January 2012.

26   Richard Schodde, "The key drivers behind resource growth: an analysis of the copper industry over the last 100 years," PowerPoint presentation to 2010 MEMS Conference Mineral and Metal Markets over the Long Term, 3 March 2010, at http://www.slideshare.net/RichardSchodde/growth-factors-for-copper-schodde-sme-mems-march-2010-final#; 0.7 percent from SNL Metals Economics Group, "SNL Metals Economics Group's copper study reveals lower grades, higher costs for copper production in 2012," at http://go.snl.com/rs/snlfinanciallc/images/MEG_CuRRS.2013_Overview.pdf?mkt_tok=3RkMMJWWfF9wsRonuaXIeu%2FhmjTEU5z16O8kXaO1hokz2EFye%2BLIHETpodcMScprN6%2BTFAwTG5toziV8R7DNLM1wy8YQWhPh

27   Thomas Graedel et al., *Recycling Rates of Metals: A Status Report*, A Report of the Working Group on Global Metal Flows (Paris: International Resource Panel, UNEP, 2011).

28   Thomas Graedel et al., *Recycling Rates of Metals: A Status Report*, A Report of the Working Group on Global Metal Flows (Paris: International Resource Panel, UNEP, 2011).

29   Thomas Graedel et al., *Recycling Rates of Metals: A Status Report*, A Report of the Working Group on Global Metal Flows (Paris: International Resource Panel, UNEP, 2011).

30   Thomas Graedel et al., *Recycling Rates of Metals: A Status Report*, A Report of the Working Group on Global Metal Flows (Paris: International Resource Panel, UNEP, 2011).

31   United States Geological Survey, "Metal Stocks in Use in the United States," Fact Sheet 2005-3090 (Reston, VA: 2005).

32   United States Geological Survey, "Metal Stocks in Use in the United States," Fact Sheet 2005-3090 (Reston, VA: 2005).

33   United States Geological Survey, "Metal Stocks in Use in the United States," Fact Sheet 2005-3090 (Reston, VA: 2005).

34   United States Geological Survey "2012 US Net Import Reliance," table in Mineral Resources Program at http://minerals.usgs.gov/

35   World Health Organization, "7 million premature deaths annually linked to air pollution," press release (Geneva: WHO, 24 March 2014) at http://www.who.int/mediacentre/news/releases/2014/air-pollution/en/

36 The European Environment: State and Outlook 2010.

37 World Health Organization, "7 million premature deaths annually linked to air pollution," press release (Geneva: WHO, 24 March 2014) at http://www.who.int/mediacentre/news/releases/2014/air-pollution/en/

38 The European Environment: State and Outlook 2010.

39 1960 dead zones from The European Environment: State and Outlook 2010; 500 dead zones from United Nations Development Programme, "Ocean Hypoxia—Dead Zones," Issue Brief at http://www.undp.org/content/dam/undp/library/Environment%20and%20Energy/Water%20and%20Ocean%20Governance/Oceans%20and%20Coastal%20Area%20Governance/OCEAN%20HYPOXIA%20ISSUE%20BRIEF.pdf

40 United Nations Environment Programme, GEO-5: Environment for a Future We Want (Nairobi: UNEP, 2012) at http://www.unep.org/geo/pdfs/geo5/GEO5_report_C6.pdf

41 United Nations Environment Programme, GEO-5: Environment for a Future We Want (Nairobi: UNEP, 2012) at http://www.unep.org/geo/pdfs/geo5/GEO5_report_C6.pdf

42 United Nations Environment Programme, GEO-5: Environment for a Future We Want (Nairobi: UNEP, 2012) at http://www.unep.org/geo/pdfs/geo5/GEO5_report_C6.pdf

43 United Nations Environment Programme, GEO-5: Environment for a Future We Want (Nairobi: UNEP, 2012) at http://www.unep.org/geo/pdfs/geo5/GEO5_report_C6.pdf

44 United Nations Environment Programme, GEO-5: Environment for a Future We Want (Nairobi: UNEP, 2012) at http://www.unep.org/geo/pdfs/geo5/GEO5_report_C6.pdf

45 United Nations Environment Programme, GEO-5: Environment for a Future We Want (Nairobi: UNEP, 2012) at http://www.unep.org/geo/pdfs/geo5/GEO5_report_C6.pdf

46 Global Footprint Network, at http://www.footprintnetwork.org/en/index.php/GFN/.

47 Global Footprint Network, at http://www.footprintnetwork.org/en/index.php/GFN/.

48 Global Footprint Network, at http://www.footprintnetwork.org/en/index.php/GFN/.

49 Global Footprint Network, at http://www.footprintnetwork.org/en/index.php/GFN/.

50 Global Footprint Network, at http://www.footprintnetwork.org/en/index.php/GFN/.

51 A.Y. Hoekstra, "Water Security of Nations: How International Trade Affects National Water Scarcity and Dependency," in Threats to Global Water Security, NATO Science for Peace and Security Series C: Environmental Security 2009, pp 27-36; at http://link.springer.com/chapter/10.1007%2F978-90-481-2344-5_3

52 USDA Production, Supply, and Distribution database, at http://apps.fas.usda.gov/psdonline/psdQuery.aspx. Grains, which form the bulk of the diet of most humans, are used as a proxy for all food.

53 Food and Agriculture Organization of the United Nations, State of Food Insecurity in the World, 2015.

54 The 1996 World Food Summit in Rome set a goal of halving the number of hungry in the world by 2015, while the Millennium Development Goals set a target of halving the proportion of hungry by 2015. One year out, the goals are hundreds of millions of people short of being met. See Hunger Notes, "Progress in reducing the number of hungry people," at http://www.worldhunger.org/articles/Learn/world%20hunger%20facts%202002.htm#Progress_in_reducing_the_number_of_hungry_people_

55 Worldwatch calculation based on: 1900 population is an average of values cited at United States Census Bureau, "Historical Estimates of World Population," at https://www.census.gov/population/international/data/worldpop/table_history.php; 2010

estimate from United Nations, Department of Economic and Social Affairs, Population Division, Population Estimates and Projections Section, online database, at *http://esa.un.org/unpd/wpp/unpp/panel_population.htm*; 2050 estimate from United Nations, op. cit. this note.

56 Nikos Alexandratos and Jelle Bruinsma, "World Agriculture Towards 2030/2050: The 2012 Revision" (Rome: FAO, June 2012) at http://www.fao.org/docrep/016/ap106e/ap106e.pdf, pp. 61 and 95.

57 FAO, "The State of Food and Agriculture," 38th Session, Rome: FAO, 15-22 June 2013 http://www.fao.org/docrep/meeting/028/mg413e.pdf

58 USDA, "USDA Agricultural Projections to 2022," February 2013 at http://www.usda.gov/oce/commodity/projections/USDAAgriculturalProjections2022.pdf

59 FAO, "The State of Food and Agriculture," 38th Session, Rome: FAO, 15-22 June 2013 http://www.fao.org/docrep/meeting/028/mg413e.pdf

60 Nikos Alexandratos and Jelle Bruinsma, "World Agriculture Towards 2030/2050: The 2012 Revision" (Rome: FAO, June 2012) at http://www.fao.org/docrep/016/ap106e/ap106e.pdf

61 U.N. Food and Agriculture Organization (FAO), Global Capture Production and Global Aquaculture Production, electronic databases, at www.fao.org/fishery/topic /16140/en, updated March 2013

62 Nikos Alexandratos and Jelle Bruinsma, "World Agriculture Towards 2030/2050: The 2012 Revision" (Rome: FAO, June 2012) at http://www.fao.org/docrep/016/ap106e/ap106e.pdf, p. 105.

63 L.R. Oldeman, et al, "World Map of the Status of Human-Induced Soil Degradation: An Explanatory Note," Global Assessment of Soil Degradation (GLASOD), International Soil Reference and Information Centre, at http://www.isric.org/sites/default/files/ExplanNote_1.pdf, and Z. G. Bai, "Proxy global assessment of land degradation," Soil Use and Management, September 2008, 24, 223–234, at http://www.geo.uzh.ch/microsite/rsl-documents/research/publications/peer-reviewed-articles/2008_Proxy-Global_SoilUseMgmt_ZB-0471031552/2008_ProxyGlobal_SoilUseMgmt_ZB.pdf

64 Z. G. Bai, "Proxy global assessment of land degradation," Soil Use and Management, September 2008, 24, 223–234, at http://www.geo.uzh.ch/microsite/rsl-documents/research/publications/peer-reviewed-articles/2008_ProxyGlobal_SoilUseMgmt_ZB-0471031552/2008_ProxyGlobal_SoilUseMgmt_ZB.pdf. Technically, the referenced study assessed change in net primary productivity, which is usually measured as the change in the mass of carbon per unit area per year, and is here called change in vegetative mass.

65 FAO, "Hot issues: water scarcity," web page at http://www.fao.org/nr/water/issues/scarcity.html

66 Nikos Alexandratos and Jelle Bruinsma, "World Agriculture Towards 2030/2050: The 2012 Revision" (Rome: FAO, June 2012) at http://www.fao.org/docrep/016/ap106e/ap106e.pdf

67 Jacob Schewe, et al, "Multimodel assessment of water scarcity under climate change," *Proceedings of the National Academy of Sciences*, 16 December 2013 at http://www.pnas.org/content/early/2013/12/12/1222460110.full.pdf+html

68 Food and Agriculture Organization of the United Nations, "Energy-Smart Food for People and Climate," 2011, at http://www.fao.org/docrep/014/i2454e/i2454e00.pdf

69   Food and Agriculture Organization of the United Nations, "Energy-Smart Food for People and Climate," 2011, at http://www.fao.org/docrep/014/i2454e/i2454e00.pdf

70   International Energy Agency, *World Energy Outlook 2013* (Paris: International Energy Agency, 2013). www.iea.org

71   Christopher B. Field, et al, "Summary for Policymakers," in *Climate Change 2014: Impacts, Adaptation, and Vulnerability, Working Group II Contribution to the Fifth Assessment Report of the Intergovernmental Panel on Climate Change* (forthcoming) at http://ipcc-wg2.gov/AR5/images/uploads/WGIIAR5-Chap5_FGDall.pdf

72   http://www.ifpri.org/sites/default/files/publications/pr21.pdf

73   C. Rosenzweig, et al, "Assessing agricultural risks of climate change in the 21st century in a global gridded crop model intercomparison," *Proc. Natl. Acad. Sci.*, doi:10.1073/pnas.1222463110, 2013.

74   J. Elliott, et al., "Constraints and potentials of future irrigation water availability on agricultural production under climate change," *Proc. Natl. Acad. Sci.*, doi:10.1073/pnas. 1222474110. 2013.

75   Marianela Fader, "Spatial decoupling of agricultural production and consumption: quantifying dependences of countries on food imports due to domestic land and water constraints," http://iopscience.iop.org/1748-9326/8/1/014046/article. See not only the article analysis but also Appendix A, which cites other studies that offer other perspectives. In addition, see Miina Porkka, et al, "From Food Insufficiency towards Trade Dependency: A Historical Analysis of Global Food Availability," PLOS ONE, December 18, 2013 at http://www.plosone.org/article/info%3Adoi%2F10.1371%2Fjournal. pone.0082714

76   Miina Porkka, et al, "From Food Insufficiency towards Trade Dependency: A Historical Analysis of Global Food Availability," PLOS ONE, December 18, 2013 at http://www.plosone.org/article/info%3Adoi%2F10.1371%2Fjournal.pone.0082714

77   United States Geological Survey, "The World's Water," http://water.usgs.gov/edu/earth wherewater.html

78   The World Bank, "As Climate Change Threatens, Water Cooperation Becomes Vital," 20 March 2013 at http://www.worldbank.org/en/news/feature/2013/03/20/ climate-change-water-cooperation

79   The World Bank, "As Climate Change Threatens, Water Cooperation Becomes Vital," 20 March 2013 at http://www.worldbank.org/en/news/feature/2013/03/20/climate-change-water-cooperation

80   Worldwatch calculations based on data in World Bank, "Renewable internal freshwater resources per capita (cubic meters)," database at http://data.worldbank.org/indica tor/ER.H2O.INTR.PC

81   Department of Economic and Social Affairs, United Nations, "International Decade for Water for Life," webpage at http://www.un.org/waterforlifedecade/scarcity.shtml

82   A.Y. Hoekstra, "Water Security of Nations: How International Trade Affects National Water Scarcity and Dependency," in Threats to Global Water Security, *NATO Science for Peace and Security Series C: Environmental Security* 2009, pp 27-36; at http://link. springer.com/chapter/10.1007%2F978-90-481-2344-5_3

83   United States Geological Survey, "The World's Water," http://water.usgs.gov/edu/ earthwherewater.html

84 UNESCO, "World's groundwater resources are suffering from poor governance, experts say," at http://www.unesco.org/new/en/natural-sciences/environment/water/single-view-fresh-water/news/worlds_groundwater_resources_are_suffering_from_poor_governance_experts_say/#.Ux55n_ldWSo

85 United Nations Environment Programme, "A Glass Half Empty: Regions at Risk Due to Groundwater Depletion: Why is this issue important?"

86 Amand Mascarelli, "Demand for water outstrips supply," *Nature* at http://www.nature.com/news/demand-for-water-outstrips-supply-1.11143

87 Katalyn A. Voss, et al., "Groundwater depletion in the Middle East from GRACE with implications for transboundary water management in the Tigris-Euphrates-Western Iran region," *Water Resources Research.*

88 Cynthia Barnett, "Groundwater Wake-up," *Ensia* (University of Minnesota), August 19, 2013, at: http://ensia.com/features/groundwater-wake-up/

89 Cynthia Barnett, "Groundwater Wake-up," *Ensia* (University of Minnesota), August 19, 2013, at: http://ensia.com/features/groundwater-wake-up/

90 Nikos Alexandratos and Jelle Bruinsma, "World Agriculture Towards 2030/2050: The 2012 Revision" (Rome: FAO, June 2012) at http://www.fao.org/docrep/016/ap106e/ap106e.pdf

91 United Nations Environment Programme, "A Glass Half Empty: Regions at Risk Due to Groundwater Depletion: Why is this issue important?"

92 Malin Falkenmark, "Growing water scarcity in agriculture: future challenge to global water security," Phil Trans R Soc A at http://www.water.ox.ac.uk/wordpress/wp-content/uploads/2013/10/Phil.-Trans.-R.-Soc.-A-2013-Falkenmark-.pdf

93 Malin Falkenmark, "Growing water scarcity in agriculture: future challenge to global water security," Phil Trans R Soc A at http://www.water.ox.ac.uk/wordpress/wp-content/uploads/2013/10/Phil.-Trans.-R.-Soc.-A-2013-Falkenmark-.pdf

94 J. Liu and H. G. Savenije, "Food consumption patterns and their effect on water requirement in China," Hydrol. Earth Syst. Sci., 12, 887-898, 2008.

95 Arjen Y. Hoekstra, "The hidden water resource use behind meat and dairy," *Animal Frontiers*, April 2012.

96 World Bank, "Water and Climate Change: Understanding the Risks and Making Climate Smart Investment Decisions," 2009 at http://www-wds.worldbank.org/external/default/WDSContentServer/WDSP/IB/2010/02/01/000333038_20100201020244/Rendered/PDF/529110NWP0Box31ge0web0large01128110.pdf

97 World Bank, "Water and Climate Change: Understanding the Risks and Making Climate Smart Investment Decisions," 2009 at http://www-wds.worldbank.org/external/default/WDSContentServer/WDSP/IB/2010/02/01/000333038_20100201020244/Rendered/PDF/529110NWP0Box31ge0web0large01128110.pdf

98 World Bank, "Water and Climate Change: Understanding the Risks and Making Climate Smart Investment Decisions," 2009 at http://www-wds.worldbank.org/external/default/WDSContentServer/WDSP/IB/2010/02/01/000333038_20100201020244/Rendered/PDF/529110NWP0Box31ge0web0large01128110.pdf

99 World Bank, "Water and Climate Change: Understanding the Risks and Making Climate Smart Investment Decisions," 2009 at http://www-wds.worldbank.org/external/default/WDSContentServer/WDSP/IB/2010/02/01/000333038_20100201020244/Rendered/PDF/529110NWP0Box31ge0web0large01128110.pdf

100 Jacob Schewe, et al., "Multimodel assessment of water scarcity under climate change," *Proceedings of the National Academy of Sciences*, 16 December 2013 at http://www.pnas.org/content/early/2013/12/12/1222460110.full.pdf+html

101 M.F. Claridge, H. A. Dawah, and M. R. Wilson (editors), *Species: The Units of Biodiversity*, (Dordrecht, Netherlands: Kluwer Academic, 1997). See also: B.A. Stein, L. S. Kutner, and J. S. Adams, *Precious Heritage: the Status of Biodiversity in the United States* (New York: Oxford University Press, 2000).

102 There may be as few as three million or as many as 100 million species on Earth, but the widely accepted estimate of 8.7 million species (not including bacteria and archaea) is documented by: C. Mora, et al., *PLoS Biology* 9, e1001127, 2011. See also summary by L. Sweetlove for *Nature* online at *http://www.nature.com/news/2011/110823/full/news.2011.498.html*

103 "Other organisms" include protists, fungi, bacteria, and archaea.

104 R. Fortey, *Life: A Natural History of the First Four Billion Years of Life on Earth* (New York: Alfred A. Knopf, 1998).

105 D. Raup and J. Sepkoski, "Periodic extinction of families and genera," *Science* 231: 833–836.

106 M.J. Benton, *When Life Nearly Died: The Greatest Mass Extinction of All Time* (London: Thames & Hudson, 2005). See also S. Sahney and Benton M.J, "Recovery from the most profound mass extinction of all time," *Proceedings of the Royal Society B* 275 (1636): 759–765. doi:10.1098/rspb.2007.1370. (2008).

107 J.R. Karr, "Health, integrity, and biological assessment: the importance of measuring whole things," in D. Pimentel, L. Westra, and R. F. Noss, eds., *Ecological Integrity: Integrating Environment, Conservation, and Health* (Washington, D.C.: Island Press, 2013).

108 B. Czech, "A chronological frame of reference for ecological integrity and natural conditions," *Natural Resources Journal* 44(4): 1113-1136, 2005.

109 Modified from: D.H. Wall, and U.N. Nielsen, "Biodiversity and ecosystem services: is it the same below ground?" *Nature Education Knowledge* 3(12): 8 2012.

110 B. Czech, P.R. Krausman, and P.K. Devers, "Economic associations among causes of species endangerment in the United States," *Bioscience* 50(7): 593-601 2000. See also: B. Czech, J.H. Mills Busa, and R.M. Brown. "Effects of economic growth on biodiversity in the United States," *Natural Resources Forum: A United Nations Sustainable Development Journal* 36 (3): 160–166) 2012.

111 B. Czech, "Economic growth as the limiting factor for wildlife conservation," *Wildlife Society Bulletin* 28(1): 4-14, 2000.

112 J. Kingdon, *Self-Made Man: Human Evolution from Eden to Extinction?* (New York: John Wiley & Sons, 1993).

113 1,519 species were listed by the U.S. Fish and Wildlife Service as threatened or endangered as of April 6, 2014. See *http://ecos.fws.gov/tess_public/pub/Boxscore.do*. A slightly greater number have been listed since passage of the Endangered Species Act because some have been delisted for various reasons (such as extinction, recovery, or mis-classification).

114 The Florida salt marsh vole comprises a relic population of the wider-spread meadow vole. It was naturally endangered by a severely restricted range, and now is also highly vulnerable to development activities, sea-level rise, and storm surges. See B. Czech, and P.R. Krausman, *The Endangered Species Act: History, Conservation Biology, and*

Public Policy. (Baltimore: Johns Hopkins University Press, 2001). See also: *http://www. fws.gov/northflorida/species-accounts/saltmarsh-vole-2005.htm* .

115 Glenn, C.R. 2006. *Earth's endangered creatures* (online). Accessed 4/6/2014 at *http:// earthsendangered.com*

116 Novacek, M.J. (editor), American Museum of Natural History (compiler),*The Biodiversity Crisis: Losing What Counts.* American Museum of Natural History Book (New York: The New Press, 2001).

117 Intergovernmental Panel on Climate Change (IPCC), Working Group II Contribution to the IPCC Fourth Assessment Report 2007: Impacts, Adaptation and Vulnerability, summarized at http://www.ipcc.ch/publications_and_data/ar4/wg2/en/ch19s19-3-4. html

118 Ridgwell, A., and D.N. Schmidt. 2010. "Past constraints on the vulnerability of marine calcifiers to massive carbon dioxide release," *Nature Geoscience*, published online February 14, 2010, doi:10.1038/ngeo755

119 World Health Organization "Nutrition: Global and regional food consumption patterns and trends: Availability and Consumption of Fish," WHO webpage at *http://www.who. int/nutrition/topics/3_foodconsumption/en/index5.html*; Food and Agriculture Organization of the United Nations, "World Review of Fisheries and Aquaculture 2012," at *http:// www.fao.org/docrep/016/i2727e/i2727e01.pdf*; United Nations, *http://www.un.org/esa/ sustdev/natlinfo/indicators/methodology_sheets/oceans_seas_coasts/pop_coastal _areas.pdf*; http://www.nature.org/ourinitiatives/habitats/oceanscoasts/explore/five-reasons-we-are-all-connected-to-oceans.xml#sthash.ky1SYQni.dpuf

120 U.N. Food and Agriculture Organization (FAO), Global Capture Production, electronic database, at www.fao.org/fishery/topic/16140/en

121 U.N. Food and Agriculture Organization (FAO), Global Capture Production, electronic database, at www.fao.org/fishery/topic/16140/en

122 Food and Agriculture Organization of the United Nations, "Review of the state of world marine fishery resources," FAO Fisheries and Aquaculture Technical Paper 569 (Rome: FAO, 2011), at http://www.fao.org/docrep/015/i2389e/i2389e.pdf

123 Food and Agriculture Organization of the United Nations, "Review of the state of world marine fishery resources," FAO Fisheries and Aquaculture Technical Paper 569 (Rome: FAO, 2011), at http://www.fao.org/docrep/015/i2389e/i2389e.pdf

124 Ransom A. Myers and Boris Worm, "Extinction, Survival or Recovery of Large Predatory Fishes," at Phil. Trans. R. Soc. B 29 January 2005 vol. 360 no. 1453 pp. 13-20.

125 Food and Agriculture Organization of the United Nations, "Review of the state of world marine fishery resources," FAO Fisheries and Aquaculture Technical Paper 569 (Rome: FAO, 2011), at http://www.fao.org/docrep/015/i2389e/i2389e.pdf

126 J.A. Anticamara, "Global fishing effort (1950–2010): Trends, gaps, and implications," *Fisheries Research*, Volume 107, Issues 1–3, January 2011, Pages 131–136.

127 Intergovernmental Panel on Climate Change (IPCC), Working Group I Contribution to the IPCC Fifth Assessment Report Climate Change 2013: The Physical Science Basis, Final Draft Underlying Scientific-Technical Assessment, September 30, 2013, at *http://www.climatechange2013.org/images/uploads/WGIAR5_WGI-12Doc2b_Final Draft_Chapter03.pdf*, p. 3-40.

128 Intergovernmental Panel on Climate Change (IPCC), Working Group I Contribution to the IPCC Fifth Assessment Report Climate Change 2013: The Physical Science

Basis, Final Draft Underlying Scientific-Technical Assessment, September 30, 2013, at *http://www.climatechange2013.org/images/uploads/WGIAR5_WGI-12Doc2b_Final Draft_Chapter03.pdf*, p. 3-6.

129 Intergovernmental Panel on Climate Change (IPCC), Working Group I Contribution to the IPCC Fifth Assessment Report Climate Change 2013: The Physical Science Basis, Final Draft Underlying Scientific-Technical Assessment, September 30, 2013, at *http://www.climatechange2013.org/images/uploads/WGIAR5_WGI-12Doc2b_FinalDraft_Chapter03.pdf*, p. 3-41.

130 Woods Hole Oceanographic Institution, "Ocean Acidification" at https://www.whoi.edu/main/topic/ocean-acidification

131 International Geosphere-Biosphere Programme, "Ocean Acidification: Summary for Policymakers," Third Symposium on the Ocean in a High CO2 World (Stockholm: IGBP, 2013) at http://www.igbp.net/download/18.30566fc6142425d6c91140a/1385975160621/OA_spm2-FULL-lorez.pdf

132 Woods Hole Oceanographic Institution, "20 Facts about Ocean Acidification," factsheet, November 2013 at http://www.whoi.edu/fileserver.do?id=165564&pt=2&p=150429

133 Galen A. McKinley, et al., "Convergence of atmospheric and North Atlantic CO2 trends on Multidecadal Timescales," *Nature Proceedings*, 8 June 2011, at *http://precedings.nature.com/documents/5993/version/1*

134 United Nations Development Programme, "Ocean Hypoxia—Dead Zones," Issue Brief at http://www.undp.org/content/dam/undp/library/Environment%20and%20Energy/Water%20and%20Ocean%20Governance/Oceans%20and%20Coastal%20Area%20Governance/OCEAN%20HYPOXIA%20ISSUE%20BRIEF.pdf

135 National Oceanic and Atmospheric Administration, Coral Reef Conservation Program, "Coral Reef Ecosystems" at http://coralreef.noaa.gov/conservation/status/

136 Mark D. Spalding, Corinna Ravilious, and Edmund P. Green, *World Atlas of Coral Reefs*, United Nations Environment Program, pp. 10 and 40.

137 National Oceanic and Atmospheric Administration, "The Value of Coral Ecosystems," at http://coralreef.noaa.gov/aboutcorals/values/

138 Justin Gillis, "U.N. Says Lag in Confronting Climate Woes Will Be Costly," *New York Times*, 16 January 2014, at http://www.nytimes.com/2014/01/17/science/earth/un-says-lag-in-confronting-climate-woes-will-be-costly.html?hp&_r=0

139 T.F. Stocker, et al., "Summary for Policymakers," in *Climate Change 2013: The Physical Science Basis*, contribution of Working Group I to the Fifth Assessment Report of the Intergovernmental Panel on Climate Change (Cambridge, UK: Cambridge University Press, 2013), at http://www.climatechange2013.org/images/report/WG1AR5_SPM_FINAL.pdf

140 M.L. Parry, *Climate Change 2007: Impacts, Adaptation and Vulnerability* contribution of Working Group II to the Fourth Assessment Report of the Intergovernmental Panel on Climate Change (Cambridge, UK: Cambridge University Press, 2013) at http://www.ipcc.ch/publications_and_data/ar4/wg2/en/ch4s4-4-11.html

141 T.F. Stocker, et al., "Summary for Policymakers," in *Climate Change 2013: The Physical Science Basis*, contribution of Working Group I to the Fifth Assessment Report of the Intergovernmental Panel on Climate Change (Cambridge, UK: Cambridge University Press, 2013), at http://www.climatechange2013.org/images/report/WG1AR5_SPM_FINAL.pdf

142   Christopher B. Field, et al., "Summary for Policymakers," in *Climate Change 2014: Impacts, Adaptation, and Vulnerability, Working Group II Contribution to the Fifth Assessment Report of the Intergovernmental Panel on Climate Change*, (forthcoming) at http://ipcc-wg2.gov/AR5/images/uploads/WGIIAR5-Chap5_FGDall.pdf

143   Christopher B. Field, et al., "Summary for Policymakers," in *Climate Change 2014: Impacts, Adaptation, and Vulnerability, Working Group II Contribution to the Fifth Assessment Report of the Intergovernmental Panel on Climate Change*, (forthcoming) at http://ipcc-wg2.gov/AR5/images/uploads/WGIIAR5-Chap5_FGDall.pdf

144   Dan Lashof and Andy Stevenson, "Who Pays for Climate Change?" NRDC Issue Paper (Washington: NRDC, May 2013) at http://www.nrdc.org/globalwarming/files/taxpayer-climate-costs-IP.pdf

145   Dan Lashof and Andy Stevenson, "Who Pays for Climate Change?" NRDC Issue Paper (Washington: NRDC, May 2013) at http://www.nrdc.org/globalwarming/files/taxpayer-climate-costs-IP.pdf

146   Tim Hume, "Report: Climate Change may pose threat to economic growth," 30 October 2013 at http://www.cnn.com/2013/10/29/world/climate-change-vulnerability-index/

147   Alister Doyle, "U.N. climate panel corrects carbon numbers in influential report," *Reuters*, 11 November 2013.

148   Justin Gillis, "U.N. Climate Panel Endorses Ceiling on Global Emissions," *New York Times*, 27 September 2013 at http://www.nytimes.com/2013/09/28/science/global-climate-change-report.html?pagewanted=all

149   Justin Gillis, "U.N. Climate Panel Endorses Ceiling on Global Emissions," *New York Times*, 27 September 2013 at http://www.nytimes.com/2013/09/28/science/global-climate-change-report.html?pagewanted=all

150   Brian Czech. *Supply Shock: Economic Growth at the Crossroads and the Steady State Solution.* (Gabriola Island, British Columbia: New Society Publishers, 2013); Rob Dietz and Dan O'Neill. *Enough Is Enough: Building a Sustainable Economy in a World of Finite Resources.* (San Francisco: Berrett-Koehler, 2013).

151   Ernst von Weizsäcker, *Factor Five: Transforming the Global Economy Through 80% Improvements in Resource Productivity* (London: Earthscan, 2009).

152   Box XX–2 from the following: USGS, "Metal Stocks in Use in the United States," Fact Sheet 2050-3090 (Reston, VA: July 2005); Ben Schiller, "Trash to Cash: Mining Landfills for Energy and Profit," *Fast Company*, 7 September 2011; Group Machiels, "Enhanced Landfill Mining," company website, at www.machiels.com/company-detail.aspx?ID=885c55e0-f3b6-4fe6-aa25-1fa7bfc312dd, viewed 23 September 2012.

153   European Commission, op. cit. note 22; UNEP, *Green Jobs: Towards Decent Work in a Sustainable, Low-carbon World* (Nairobi: 2008).

154   Office of the Mayor, "Mayor Lee Celebrates San Francisco's Composting Achievements," press release (San Francisco: 28 March 2012); United States from U.S. Environmental Protection Agency (EPA), *Municipal Solid Waste Generation, Recycling, and Disposal in the United States: Facts and Figures for 2010* (Washington, DC: 2011); Barbara K. Reck and T. E. Graedel, "Challenges in Metal Recycling," *Science*, 10 August 2012.

155   Table X from the following: Elliot Martin, Susan A. Shaheen, and Jeffrey Lidi, "Impact of Carsharing on Household Vehicle Holdings: Results from North American

Shared-Use Vehicle Survey," *Transportation Research Record*, March 2010; John A. Mathews and Hao Tan, "Progress Toward a Circular Economy in China: The Drivers (and Inhibitors) of Eco-industrial Initiative," *Journal of Industrial Ecology*, June 2011, pp. 435–57; U.S. Department of Energy and EPA, *Combined Heat and Power: A Clean Energy Solution* (Washington, DC: August 2012); Eric S. Belsky, "Planning for Inclusive and Sustainable Urban Development," in Worldwatch Institute, *State of the World 2012* (Washington, DC: Island Press, 2012), p. 45; "Neighborhood Tool Libraries in Portland Oregon," at www.neighborhoodnotes.com/directory/category/community_and_social_services/neighborhood_tool_libraries, viewed 23 September 2012; Osamu Kimura, *Japanese Top Runner Approach for Energy Efficiency Standards*, SERC Discussion Paper 09035 (Tokyo: Socio-economic Research Center, Central Research Institute of Electric Power Industry, 2010).

156   Brian Czech. *Shoveling Fuel for a Runaway Train* (San Francisco: University of California Press, 2000).

INDEX